ADVANCE PRAISE FOR

Preaching During a Pandemic: The Rhetoric of the Black Preaching Tradition, Volume I

Directly in line with the long tradition of African American preaching that brings hope, justice, and healing, these volumes curate sermons that are theologically rich and rhetorically creative, offering insights into contemporary and relevant preaching around social justice, COVID-19, and health disparities in America. An absolute must-read!!!!

—Frank A. Thomas, Director of the Ph.D. Program in African American Preaching and Sacred Rhetoric, Christian Theological Seminary

This intergenerational, interdenominational compilation shows forth the multi-vocality of Black preaching, the vastness of our theological imagination, and the richness of our rhetorical genius. Ultimately, this compilation draws our attention to the greatest powers of Black preaching in times of upheaval: to help God's people make meaning of our lived experiences, to return to the transgenerational theological truths that have held our people together, and to give voice to the new things that God is saying and doing in our lifetimes.

—Neichelle Guidry, Dean of Sisters Chapel, Spellman College

Our most elegant preachers and theological thinkers remind us that the Divine exists in community. Likewise, they also remind us that preachers do not pro-claim the gospel in isolation. What the pandemic(s) of 2020 reminded us of is that we are surrounded by a great cloud of contemporary witnesses whose gifts, struggles, and hermeneutical acumen can strengthen our own. Those who preach and love preaching are presented as colleagues and able craftspersons of sacred rhetoric in this well-curated volume. Preachers, the pandemics are not over. We cannot survive them homiletically by ourselves. Read these sermons.

—William H. Lamar IV, Pastor, Metropolitan African Methodist Episcopal Church, Washington, DC

The last few years of COVID-19, Black Lives Matter protests, and political upheaval has left Black folx betwixt and between multiple crises in the village, all streaming live for the consumption of a global audience. Yet, beyond a rhetorical geography rifled with strange fruit, this timely text captures the prophetic prowess and anointed adroitness of Black preachers who take up their pulpits to meet their communities where they are—and still find a way to lead them toward hope everlasting.

—Dianna Watkins Dickerson, Chaplain, United States Air Force and President of the African American Communication and Culture Division of the National Communication Association

Preaching During a Pandemic

Studies in Communication, Culture, Race, and Religion

Andre E. Johnson
Series Editor

Vol. 1

The Studies in Communication, Culture, Race, and Religion series is part
of the Peter Lang Media and Communication list.
Every volume is peer reviewed and meets
the highest quality standards for content and production.

PETER LANG
New York • Bern • Brussels • Lausanne • Oxford

Preaching During a Pandemic

The Rhetoric of the Black Preaching Tradition, Volume I

Edited by
Andre E. Johnson, Kimberly P. Johnson, and
Wallis C. Baxter III

PETER LANG
New York • Bern • Brussels • Lausanne • Oxford

Library of Congress Cataloging-in-Publication Data

Names: Johnson, Andre E., editor. | Johnson, Kimberly P., editor. | Baxter, Wallis C., III,
editor.
Title: Preaching during a pandemic: the rhetoric of the Black preaching tradition /
edited by Andre E. Johnson, Kimberly P. Johnson, Wallis C. Baxter, III.
Description: New York: Peter Lang, 2023.
Series: Studies in communication, culture, race, and religion; vol. 1–2
ISSN 2834-7013 (print) | ISSN 2771-4543 (online)
Includes bibliographical references.
Identifiers: LCCN 2022029417 (v. 1; print) | LCCN 2022029418 (v. 1; ebook) |
ISBN 978-1-4331-8617-2 (v. 1; hardback) | ISBN 978-1-4331-8635-6 (v. 1; paperback) |
ISBN 978-1-4331-8618-9 (v. 1; ebook pdf) | ISBN 978-1-4331-8619-6 (v. 1; epub)
LCCN 2022029497 (v. 2; print) | ISBN 978-1-4331-8752-0 (v. 2; hardback) |
ISBN 978-1-4331-8753-7 (v. 2; paperback) | ISBN 978-1-4331-8754-4 (v. 2; ebook pdf) |
ISBN 978-1-4331-8755-1 (v. 2; epub)
Subjects: LCSH: Sermons, American—African American authors. | COVID-19
(Disease)—Religious aspects—Christianity. | Bible—Sermons.
Classification: LCC BV4241.5 .P69 (print) | LCC BV4241.5 (ebook) |
DDC 252.0089/96073—dc23/eng/20221014
LC record available at https://lccn.loc.gov/2022029417
LC ebook record available at https://lccn.loc.gov/2022029418
DOI 10.3726/b18146 (v. 1)
DOI 10.3726/b19954 (v. 2)

Bibliographic information published by **Die Deutsche Nationalbibliothek.**
Die Deutsche Nationalbibliothek lists this publication in the "Deutsche
Nationalbibliografie"; detailed bibliographic data are available
on the Internet at http://dnb.d-nb.de/.

Table of Contents

Acknowledgments

In addition to thanking our families, friends, colleagues, and supporters, we would like to thank Niall Kennedy, Joshua Charles, and the good people at Peter Lang Publishing for their work in bringing this project to fruition. We would also like to thank Michael Gipson, who started this project with us, and for the Studies in Communication, Culture, Race, and Religion book series. We also would like to thank the contributors for their submissions and patience as we put this book together during a pandemic. We also thank the Black Church for still finding ways out of no way to serve and minister to the people of God.
Andre
Kimberly
Wallis

Introduction: The Rhetoric of the Black Pulpit: The Collection of Black Sermons

With this project, our aims are simple. While like others before us, we understand and appreciate the Black preacher's role in the history of the United States. From enslavement workcamps to time spent in hush harbors, the Black preacher managed somehow to inspire, encourage, and equip those shacked within the American slavocracy. This oratorical tradition carried African Americans through Reconstruction, the Harlem Renaissance, Jim and Jane Crow, the Civil Rights Movement, the Black Power Movement, the Black Arts Movement, and the #BlackLivesMatter Movement.

Though the Black preacher was called upon to speak truth and triumph amid varied seasons of the human plight in America, COVID-19 and the politics of a pandemic made this a different moment in American history. We suggest that this moment was different and significant because many churches did not meet physically. More specifically, the comfort of companionship and collective comradery that the Black Church provided for its members was gone in an instant. Even during slavery, even in secret, the church met physically, so for many worshippers, this was new terrain. How does one preach while navigating a pandemic? How does one worship? How does one minister with music? What about the outreach ministries and other ministries that churches do—how do we do them in the middle of a pandemic became questions all church leaders and congregants ask of themselves.

Therefore, in that tension, we called for sermons for a two-volume set titled *Preaching During a Pandemic: The Rhetoric of the Black Preaching Tradition*. We envisioned this book to be a collection of sermons from those who preach within the Black preaching tradition. By publishing these sermons, we hope to address questions: what were those who preached in the Black preaching tradition sharing with their congregants? How were they incorporating and infusing COVID-19 in their sermons? What shape did the prophetic and priestly sermon take when preaching during a pandemic? Were specific models or types of sermons—womanist, prophetic/liberation, narrative, contemplative, celebrative, expository, thematic, induction, deductive—more frequently employed during a crisis? We aimed to collect some of the best sermons of the Black Preaching Tradition during this COVID-19 pandemic.

The collection and publication of African American sermons have been the foundation of the understanding and the appreciation of the African American rhetoric and public address tradition. One of the first collections of sermons from a Black preacher was Episcopalian Alexander Crummell in 1862. Titled *The Future of Africa: Addresses and Sermons Delivered in the Republic of Liberia*, the volume consisted of speeches and sermons delivered while he served as Minister to Liberia for the United States government. Texts in this collection centered on the "interests of Africa and the Negro race" and performed two important ends. First, Crummell, through his oratory and preaching, wanted to show that the "children of Africa" had been "called in Divine Providence to meet the demand of civilization" and second, to demonstrate that they have already started to "grapple with the problems which pertain to the responsible manhood."[1]

In 1884, another early collection of sermons came from J. W. Hood titled, *The Negro in the Christian Pulpit; or the Two Characters and Two Destinies as Delineated in Twenty-One Practical Sermons*. This collection differed from Crummell's in two significant ways. First, Hood includes an introductory chapter written by a white minister, Atticus G. Haygood, who served as president of Emory College. In the introduction, Haygood offered a brief bio sketch of Hood and vouched for his "high character."[2]

Second, Hood included sermons from other ministers within his denomination, AMEZ (African Methodist Episcopal Zion) church. Not only would this be one of, if not the first collection of sermons from an AMEZ minister, but also

---

1 Alexander Crummell, *The Future of Africa: Addresses, Sermons, Etc., Etc., Delivered in the Republic of Liberia*. New York: Charles Scribner Publisher, 1862, 3–4.

2 J. W. Hood, *The Negro in the Christian Pulpit; or the Two Characters and Two Destinies as Delineated in Twenty-One Practical Sermons*. Raleigh: Edwards, Broughton & Co. Steam Power Printers and Binders, 1884, 3.

one of the first collections of sermons that included sermons from someone else other than the author of the collection.

For his part, Hood outlined three reasons why he published this work. First, he noted the shortage of a collection of sermons from a "colored Methodist minister," and he reasoned that it was time for someone to offer a "sample of their pulpit deliverances in the form of a book for public criticism." Second, candidates had to read sermons as part of their ordination process, Black preachers should produce sermons for candidates to read, and third, many had urged him to publish his sermons.[3]

In 1890, Edward M. Brawley edited *The Negro Baptist Pulpit: A Collection of Sermons and Papers on Baptist Doctrine and Missionary and Educational Work*. This work featured a who's who of nineteenth-century Baptist ministers, including Emmanuel K. Love,[4] William J. Simmons,[5] and Solomon T. Clanton.[6] However, this collection is noteworthy because Brawley included a sermon from Mary V. Cook[7] titled "The Work for Baptist Women." At the time, Cook served as the Professor of Latin Language and Literature at State University (now Kentucky State) in Louisville, Kentucky. To our knowledge, this volume has the distinction of being the first collection of sermons to feature a sermon by a Black woman.

Colored (Christian) Methodist Episcopal (CME) Bishop Lucius Henry Holsey, in 1898, published a collection of sermons titled *Autobiography, Sermons, Addresses, and Essays*. Holsey published his work with the hope not only to "disseminate the truths and glory of the gospel system" but also to inspire African Americans to think and to "encourage investigation, literary advancement, and authorship" by people of his race.[8]

After 1900, however, sermon publications from Black preachers began to decline.[9] One reason for this perhaps was the focus on the African American

---

3 Hood, *The Negro in the Christian Pulpit*, 7.

4 Emmanuel K. Love (1850–1900) was pastor of First African Baptist Church in Savannah, Georgia, the oldest Black church in North America.

5 Williams J. Simmons (1849–1890) served as the District Secretary of the American Baptist Home Mission and in 1880, became president of Kentucky Normal and Theological Institute (now Simmons College in Kentucky.

6 Solomon T. Clanton (1857–1918) served as the Missionary of the American Baptist Publication Society for Louisiana and later became a professor at Alabama A&M and briefly served as its president.

7 Mary V. Cook (1862–1945).

8 Lucius H. Holsey, *Autobiography, Sermons, Addresses and Essays*. Atlanta: The Franklin Printing and Publishing Company. 1898, 3–4.

9 Two notable exceptions were W. Bishop Johnson's The Scourging of a Race and other Sermons and Addresses. (Washington, D.C.: Murray Brothers Printing Co., 1904) and Carter G. Woodson, ed., The Works of Francis J. Grimke (Washington, D.C.: Associated Publishers, 1942).

public address tradition as a whole. In other words, instead of focusing on sermons, especially with the publication of Carter G. Woodson's *Negro Orators and Their Orations*, many were now interested in speeches and public addresses outside of the pulpit. Black scholars, in particular, began doing what we now call "rhetorical history." They also began to turn their attention to "African American folk language and how folk language helped shape American culture." They examined African Americans' systems regarding the "teaching and training for oratory and debate."[10]

An example of this was AME Bishop Reverdy Ransom. Instead of publishing a book of his sermons, he decided to publish a book of his public addresses titled, *The Spirit of Freedom and Justice: Orations and Speeches*.[11] As Johnson noted in his overview of the Black public address tradition, "many of the speeches reproduced for the volume were epideictic, as he celebrated the likes of William Lloyd Garrison, Abraham Lincoln, John Brown, and Charles Sumner."[12] The book also received rave reviews. Alain Locke suggested in a book review that Ransom's work would profit "anyone interested in studying the mind of the Negro as a reaction to his treatment in America."[13]

Perhaps there was also another reason for the change. Again, as Johnson noted:

African Americans had been studying in academic settings the art of speech and debate since the founding of HBCUs in this country and that master's and doctoral theses examined black rhetorical history and forms in unique and valuable ways that offered new concepts and frameworks for understanding black speech. They also improved on existing ones by including black voices and providing the historical context that Woodson would agree was important to any analysis. In short, African American scholars also began to interpret for themselves this valuable material. No longer would they be comfortable in allowing white scholars to interpret or nullify the black experience. They would argue that the black experience was valuable and the texts that scholars discovered were also worthy of study.[14]

Whatever may have been the reason, outside of a few additional books, volumes of sermons from African American preachers were exceedingly rare.

---

10 Andre E. Johnson, "My Sanctified Imagination: Carter G. Woodson and a Speculative (Rhetorical) History of African American Public Address, 1926–1960," *Rhetoric and Public Affairs*, Spring-Summer 2021, Vol 24, No 1–2, p. 15–50, 38–39.

11 Reverdy Ransom, *The Spirit of Freedom and Justice: Orations and Speeches*. Nashville, TN: AME Sunday School Union, 1926.

12 Johnson, "My Sanctified Imagination," 32.

13 Alain Locke, "Review: The Spirit of Freedom and Justice: Orations and Speeches," *Journal of Negro History* 12 (1927): 99.

14 Johnson, "My Sanctified Imagination," 39.

However, this began to change in the 1970s. Benefitting from the Black Power and Black Studies movements, Henry Mitchell's scholarship and the publication of his foundational book, Black Preaching, scholars of both homiletics and Black public address (re)turn to the collections of sermons. One of the first ones, published in 1972, was William M. Philpot's *Best Black Sermons*. In the introduction, famed preacher Gardner C. Taylor wrote that the sermons in this volume would "illustrate the vitality of the black church and the centrality of preaching which still characterize this principal institution in America."[15] Selected by an advisory panel led by Philpot and Taylor,[16] the volume included sermons from noted Black preachers such as Martin Luther King Jr., Benjamin E. Mays, Otis Moss Jr., Kelly Miller Smith, Hosea Williams, and Gayraud S. Wilmore.

Other books consisting of Black sermons would soon follow. In 1973, Manuel L. Scott published *The Gospel for the Ghetto: Sermons from the Black Pulpit*. In this volume, Scott wanted to "acknowledge the need to accent and amplify those portions of the Christian proclamation that the thinking and believing poor welcome as good news."[17] In 1976, Alfred J. Smith published *Outstanding Black Sermons*. This title became so popular that others published their collection of Black sermons under the same title. In 1977, Robert T. Newbold published *Black Preaching: Select Sermons in the Presbyterian Tradition*.[18] As the title suggests, the volume consists of sermons from Black Presbyterian preachers. However, unlike the previous books, *Black Preaching* includes women preachers. Out of the twenty-one sermons included in the volume, four are from women, including womanist pioneer Katie G. Cannon.

In 1985, Ella Pearson Mitchell would include Cannon and thirteen others in editing the groundbreaking volume *Those Preaching Women: Sermons by Black Women Preachers*.[19] *Those Preaching Women* has the distinction of being the first collection of sermons by Black women. In a review of the book, Renita J. Weems noted that "by bringing together these fine sermons from some of the finest Black women preachers from across the country, Dr. Mitchell has initiated a coup against the past sins of History and the Church." The volume resonated so much

---

15   Gardner C. Taylor, "Introduction," in *Best Black Sermons*. Valley Forge, P A: Judson Press, 1972, 6.

16   Other members of the panel were Walter B. Hoard, Colin W. Williams, and Samuel W. Winslow.

17   Manuel L. Scott, ed., *The Gospel for the Ghetto: Sermons from a Black Pulpit*. Nashville: Broadman Press, 1973, ix.

18   Robert T. Newbold, ed., *Black Preaching: Select Sermons in the Presbyterian Tradition*. Louisville: Geneva Press, 1977.

19   Ella Pearson Mitchell, *Those Preaching Women: Sermons by Black Women Preachers*. Valley Forge, PA: Judson Press, 1985.

with the Black Church and the broader public that Mitchell would publish five volumes in this series.[20]

In 1997, the Black preaching tradition would receive even more attention with the publication of the *African American Pulpit*. Initially founded by David Albert Farmer, a white minister who pastored University Baptist Church in Baltimore, he designed the journal with the Black preacher in mind. Farmer, who had long been "attracted by the power and beauty of Black preaching," gave his reason for starting the journal. He said, "there never has been a magazine (journal) for Black preachers, either to emphasize it or to help black preachers prepare sermons by giving them ideas or showing them what their colleagues are doing." He later invited Kirk Byron Jones to co-edit the journal, and they released the first issue in November. Listed as the Winter/Spring 1997–1998 issue, it featured nine sermons.[21]

In 2000, Martha Simmons and Frank A. Thomas would take over as co-editors of the journal. Building on the success and continued growth of the "African American Pulpit," in 2001, Martha Simmons and Frank A. Thomas published *9.11.01: African American Leaders Respond to An American Tragedy*. Though as Simmons noted in the book, in "times of terror, the African American pulpit has spoken with its clearest voice,"[22] this volume is unique in that it was the first published sermon collection from Black preachers in response to a specific American event. In their review of the book, *Publishers Weekly* wrote that this "collection is everything that most other books on September 11 have tried but failed."[23] They called the sermons and essays in the book "cogent, piercing, inspirational, and gritty."[24]

Simmons and Thomas' collaboration would continue in 2010 with the foundational text "Preaching with Sacred Fire: An Anthology of African American Sermons, 1750 to the Present." With over one hundred sermons, it has the distinction of being the largest single volume of Black sermons. In producing the anthology, Simmons and Thomas wanted to achieve four things. First, they wanted to "place a record of several hundred years of Black preaching in one volume to maintain for posterity a reader on Black preaching." Second, they wanted

---

20 Renita J. Weems, Those Preaching Women: Sermons by Black Women Preachers (Review). Sage. Vol 3 Issue 2, (Fall, 1986): 56

21 New Journal Highlights Work of Black Preachers, *Tampa Bay Times*, November 8, 1997. https://www.tampabay.com/archive/1997/11/08/new-journal-highlights-work-of-black-preachers/.

22 Martha Simmons and Frank A. Thomas, 9.11.01: African American Leaders Respond to An American tragedy. Valley Forge: Judson Press, X.

23 9.11.01: African American Leaders Respond to an American Tragedy. *Publishers Weekly*, December 1, 2001. https://www.publishersweekly.com/978-0-8170-1435-3.

24 Ibid.

to "document the richness and variety of the preaching produced by African Americans." Third, they wanted to "expand the world's understanding of Black preaching to demonstrate how it has provided orators whose words have enhanced the human landscape." Finally, they wanted to extend a "clarion call" to institutions of higher education to "establish permanent facilities, to collect, house, analyze, interpret and preserve the preaching legacy" of Black preaching.

Simmons and Thomas seem to have achieved their goals. Since the publication of *Sacred Fire*, there has been more attention paid to the African American preaching tradition across several different disciplines. The number of books, articles, conferences, programs, and dissertations attest to this. However, with all this robust attention being paid to the Black preaching tradition, since 2010, there has not been any significant collection of Black sermons, and we wanted to change that.

In the first volume collection, we collect some of the best sermons from the Hebrew Bible or the Old Testament. Ristina Gooden in her sermon, "What Happens in the Wilderness" (Genesis 16:7–13 NRSV) focuses on the wilderness experience and how we can reimagine the space as a starting place for liberation and freedom.

In her sermon, "Do Not Pass Me By" (Exodus 11:4–8 NRSV), Heather S. Wills preaches about the series of plagues released on the land of Egypt to show us that "even when there is destruction, chaos, turmoil, inequitable treatment, and even death, God is still present" and God still protects us. Also from the book of Exodus, Jamar Boyd II in "Surviving Quarantine" (Exodus 12:13, 22–23; Ephesians 3:16–19 NIV), likening the 2020 pandemic to the experiences of the Israelites in the book of Exodus. Boyd then offers three ways to survive during our moments of quarantine: apply the solution, adhere to the command, and await the relief.

Donna Vanhook in "Hope in the Holla" (Numbers 27:1–5, NRSV), draws from the story of Zelophehad's daughters, the ones who fought against tradition to petition for their father's inheritance. She reminds us that "God can change tradition; God can make provisions for changing policy." Vanhook proclaims, "With one Holla, case law was established for these young women giving us hope today that taking a stand can yield transformation."

In "The Ministry of Manna" (Deuteronomy 8:1–5 NRSV), Howard-John Wesley highlights our uncertainty surrounding COVID-19 and likens it to the journey of the Israelites while in the wilderness. While the wilderness is a place of uncertainty, fear and doubt, Wesley reminds us that God is still there guiding us to through all of our insecurities.

Wallis C. Baxter III in "What Does All of this Mean" (Joshua 4:5–7, ESV), draws from the story of Joshua telling the men from each tribe to collect 12 stones from the Jordan river. The scripture tells us that future generations will ask, what do those stones mean? Similarly, Baxter poses the question, what does all of this mean? In Joshua's words to the Israelites, he reminds us that "life is significant, our legacy is secure and that liberation is sufficient" because "God always comes through."

In the first of four sermons drawing from the book of Psalms, Tamara O. Kersey, in "Remembering God in Troubled Times" (Psalm 20:6–8 NKJV) reminds us that we must stay focused and trust God in troubled times. For her, we must not only remember God, but we must also remember and know who God is. It is in seasons of strife and struggle that Kersey reminds us not to draw primarily from our own strength and wisdom, but from the wisdom and hope in God.

In "Singing Without a Sanctuary" (Psalm 27:4–6, NASB), Aaron Marble, draws from the structural fire that happened on April 15, 2019, at the iconic Notre Dame Cathedral to remind us that we can still sing without a sanctuary. Although COVID-19 has forced many churches to close their doors to public worship, we do not have to gather in a church to sing praises unto God. He tells us, "We have reasons to sing even without a sanctuary."

In "Pandemic Loneliness" (Psalm 66:8–20; John 14:15–21 NRSV), Andre E. Johnson preaches about spiritual loneliness during a pandemic. While not ideal, he also suggests that this longing can reignite and strengthen us as we continue our journeys. Glencie Rhedrick in "What's Going On" (Psalm 82:1–6), challenges pastors, preachers, and all church leaders to see this epidemic as a chance to renew their calls to "justice, fairness, and equality."

R. Janae Pitts-Murdock, in her sermon "I Can't Breathe" (Isaiah 40: 27–29 NASB), focuses on the prophet Isaiah offering comfort to the people of Israel. Pitts-Murdock reminds us that even when it feels "like our way is hidden from the LORD, and the justice due us escapes the notice of God, God's got time," "God's understanding is inscrutable," "God gives strength to the weary," and "God increases power to the one who lacks might."

In "Building Houses in Babylon" (Jeremiah 29:4–11, NKJV), C. Dexter Wise III positions the pandemic as a time of upheaval and change. Drawing from the exilic conditions suffered by Judah, Wise III warns us that in seasons of upheaval and change, who we listen to is important. Grounded in the godly counsel of Jeremiah, he suggests we can do four things while waiting on our change to come.

In "How Long? We Can't Breathe" (Habakkuk 1:2), arguing that we have "double pneumonia," Cory Jones asks the question of "how long" against the backdrop of the pandemic and racism. By incorporating themes from Pentecost Sunday, Jones reminds us that when we can't breathe, God breathes on us. We end with a poem from Patricia Robinson Williams titled "Lines Written Upon Reflection on Contemporary Moral Decay."

What Happens in the Wilderness?: Genesis 16:7–13 (NRSV)

RISTINA GOODEN

August 2, 2020

7 The angel of the Lord found her by a spring of water in the wilderness, the spring on the way to Shur.8 And he said, "Hagar, slave-girl of Sarai, where have you come from and where are you going?" She said, "I am running away from my mistress Sarai." 9 The angel of the Lord said to her, "Return to your mistress, and submit to her." 10 The angel of the Lord also said to her, "I will so greatly multiply your offspring that they cannot be counted for multitude." 11 And the angel of the Lord said to her, "Now you have conceived and shall bear a son; you shall call him Ishmael, for the Lord has given heed to your affliction. 12 He shall be a wild ass of a man, with his hand against everyone, and everyone's hand against him; and he shall live at odds with all his kin." 13 So she named the Lord who spoke to her, "You are El-roi"; for she said, "Have I really seen God and remained alive after seeing him?"

Beloved, I would like to spend these next few moments focusing on the topic:

> What Happens in the Wilderness
> In preparing for this sermon,
> I desperately tried to find a modern-day movie example of a
>   black woman running away from her life and wandering
>   the world trying to find herself.
> Something similar to Eat, Pray, Love
> but instead of starring Julia Roberts,

It would star Gabrielle Union, Samira Wiley, or Lizzo.
Imagine one those stunning black women
embarking on a silent retreat,
eating her way through Wakanda,
and meeting a palm reader in Bali.
It's unfortunate that I struggled to find such a movie.
But we know plenty of folks who found themselves in the wilderness.
The wilderness of a failed job, business, or relationship.
The wilderness of poverty.
The wilderness of trauma.
The wilderness of a pandemic.

The wilderness of being Black or brown in a world desperately trying to cling to its whiteness.

We know black women who have been in the wilderness.
Harriet Tubman.
Ida B. Wells-Barnett.
Diane Nash.
Katherine Johnson.
Angela Davis.
Assata Shakur.
Maya Angelou.
Maybe even yourself.
And also, Hagar.
Hagar,
for those of you who struggled to find Genesis,
is the Egyptian slave of Sarah, wife of Abraham.
Abraham and Sarah had been married for quite some time but did not have children.

In Chapter 15 God had promised Abraham that he would have more descendants than stars in the sky.

Abraham and Sarah, unclear how that would happen in their ripe old age, took matters into their own hands.

Chapter 16, verse 4 says that Abraham went into Hagar, and she conceived.

We can all figure out what that means, and we will have to talk about consent on another day.

Now that Hagar was pregnant by Abraham, Sarah has an attitude.

She felt like Hagar had become uppity now that she was pregnant.

Abraham, trying to abide by happy wife, happy life, tells Sarah to do as she pleases with Hagar.

The text says that Sarah dealt with Hagar harshly.

Isn't that some... nonsense?

Sarah forced Hagar into this situation and is dealing with her harshly for how things turned out.

Again, another story for another day.

So, Hagar runs away to the wilderness and that is where we find her in this text.

Hagar, a single, Black, pregnant woman, is in the wilderness alone when an angel of the Lord appears to her.

The wilderness.

The wilderness appears nearly 300 times in the Bible.

We often see reference to the wilderness throughout the Old and New Testament when folks are searching for the Promised Land or encountering God.

Wilderness when translated from the Hebrew root means to push out and drive away.

The wilderness.

God takes us through the wilderness so that we can hear God and allow God to push something out of us.

Even Jesus goes to the wilderness in Matthew 4.

In that wilderness experience, Jesus' tempter challenges him to call on God to turn the rocks into bread.

Jesus answered, "It is written: 'Man shall not live on bread alone, but on every word that comes from the mouth of God.'"

We see that same language in Deuteronomy 8:3 when the Israelites are in the wilderness.

One does not live by bread alone, but by every word that comes from the mouth of the Lord.

What are you living on in your wilderness?

I know what you are thinking.

Can't God just work on me on Sundays between 10:45 am and 12 pm so I have time to make it to brunch?

The answer is no.

In the wilderness,

when you are all by yourself,

running from whatever is behind you,

in the most trying moments of your life,

3 things happen that make the journey necessary.

First thing that happens is that you find yourself.

When the angel appears to Hagar, the angel calls her slave-girl of Sarai.

We know that what your job is,

Or the company you keep

or in some cases the family that you come from,

but that does not always define who you are.

What defines you is how you make it through.

How do you respond to adversity and show persistence?

Know that finding yourself does not always mean letting go of the past.

I recently learned about Sankofa.

It's a Ghanaian word that means reaching back to knowledge gained in the past and bringing it into the present in order to make positive progress.

The old saints say, "When I look back over my life."

Sankofa.

Use the past to make positive steps forward.

But how can you do that without having seen God?

No, not literally, with your eyes but see God...

in action, in nature, in life...

that wind that whispers to you...

that tugging in your spirit.

That's God telling you to keep going.

In verse 13, Hagar said, "Have I really seen God and remained alive after seeing him?"

When you walk through the wilderness, you start to realize how strong and powerful you are.

You realize you have agency.

You realize your voice matters.

You realize the color of your skin or the body you have should not determine how people treat you.

The wilderness will teach you all about yourself.

Second and likely the most important thing that happens in the wilderness is that You find God.

Hagar is at her wit's end when God appears to her.

She was enslaved,

Raped by her master's husband for the purpose of having children.

Then cruelly mistreated for getting pregnant.

Her personhood was being ignored.

Every day she woke up to a life that was not of her own making.

She was just a walking womb.

But in the wilderness, God sees her.

Hagar is the only person in the Bible to name God.

Not Adam.

Not Abraham.

Not Moses.

Not David.

A single, Black, pregnant woman is the ONLY person in the entire Bible to name God.

And she names God

El-ROI

The God who sees me.

If you have been through a wilderness or two, you know that folks can't tell you who God is.

You have to experience God and figure it out for yourself.

You see,

You don't call God Jehovah Jireh if God has not provided the last $500 you needed to pay your rent.

You can't see God as Jehovah Rapha if God has not healed your shattered heart.

You don't call God Jehovah Nissi if God did not shelter you from the true consequences of a poor life choice that should have left you in jail or dead.

And you definitely don't call God El-Roi if God has not seen you in your darkest moments and spoken life and life more abundantly.

But God can be whatever you need God to be.

God can be he, she, they, whoever.

Everyone's God does not need to look the same.

In the wilderness, you find God. You name God. And you begin to take the next steps with God.

So, you are wandering through the wilderness and you have found God and you have found yourself.

The third and final thing that happens is that you find your purpose.

Read verse 9 & 10 again.

The angel of the Lord said to her, "Return to your mistress, and submit to her."

The angel of the Lord also said to her, "I will so greatly multiply your offspring that they cannot be counted for multitude."

God is sending Hagar back to her mistress.

I know that feels disrespectful.

But if we read further into this, we see that God has a plan for Hagar and she's going back different than the way she came.

Oh, beloved, what happens when we show up brand new in old spaces?

Hagar returned with a promise.

What will you return with?

Hagar's promise from God was not only that she would give birth to a child that would live.

But she too, would live.

This pericope took place quite a few millennia ago.

The number of women who died during childbirth was high.

It's 2020 and Black women are STILL 3–4 times more likely to die during childbirth than our white counterparts.

So, what's happening now was happening then.

God not only told Hagar that she and her child would survive the delivery,

But then God promised her the same promise that God had promised Abraham.

That she will have more offspring than she could count.

Imagine that classic children's song, Father Abraham.

You know,

The one with many sons,

And many sons had Father Abraham.

I am one of them.

And so are you.

So, let's just praise the Lord.

Then you stomp your right or left foot as hard as you can.

Same song can be sung for Hagar.

Mother Hagar

Had a son.

And that son had sons, daughters, and non-binary children.

I, too, am one of them.

And so are you.

So, let's swag surf or something.

I imagine Hagar singing Beyonce in the wilderness when she heard this news.

"My great-great-grandchildren already rich. That's a lot of brown chil'ren on your Forbes list."

Hagar's time in the wilderness is not in vain.

And your time in the wilderness isn't either.

Remember when we all pledged that 2020 was our year?

We all suddenly had 20/20 vision.

For two good months we were well on our way.

Then a pandemic hit.

Suddenly, unless you were essential, you were working from home.

Next our economy came tumbling down.

Working from home suddenly became just being at home, likely with kids who were trying to adjust to this new reality.

Then Ahmaud Arbury, George Floyd, Breonna Taylor, Tony McDade, David Mcatee, Rayshard Brooks and the countless names that we know and don't know.

We marched in the streets, willing to risk our lives for the justice we deserve.

No Justice. No Peace.

Buildings were burned, monuments were torn down.

No Justice. No Peace.

Police showed up in riot gear. They showed up unmarked. They tear gassed protestors and white moms alike.

No Justice. No Peace.

But in the words of the late John Lewis, "When historians pick up their pens to write the story of the 21st century, let them say that it was your generation who laid down the heavy burdens of hate at last and that peace finally triumphed over violence, aggression and war."[25]

For many of us, this is the wilderness, but our ancestors walked this path before.

We must realize that God is the one that chose us for such a time as this.

We may wake up some mornings trying to figure out who thought this was a good idea,

Quit 5 times before we have our first sip of coffee,

And try to see how we can gain dual citizenship in Canada,

But then God steps in and reminds us that we belong in this space and even more importantly in this country.

The historians will remember the Black women that put this country on their backs and carried us to a better tomorrow.

Bozoma Saint John
Eboni Marshall Turman
Michelle Alexander
Patrisse Cullors
Raquel Willis
Tabitha Brown
Tarana Burke
And yes, still even you.

So even if you are falling apart, remember that God is trying to push something out of you.

In the wilderness you find your voice to write your own story.

So, keep standing.

Keep fighting your way through.

Remember Sankofa.

Find yourself, find God, find your purpose.

This wilderness may allow you to start a business, break a generational curse, or stir up a movement.

God wants to work through you just like God worked through a single, pregnant, enslaved Egyptian woman.

The Book of Mormon says, "And I will also be your light in the wilderness; and I will prepare the way before you."[26]

May you always remember what happens in the wilderness.

25   John Lewis, "Together, You Can Redeem the Soul of Our Nation," *New York Times*, July 30, 2020. https://www.nytimes.com/2020/07/30/opinion/john-lewis-civil-rights-america.html
26   1 Nephi 17:13.

Do Not Pass Me By: Exodus 11: 4–8 (NRSV)

HEATHER S. WILLS

May 8, 2020

Moses said, "Thus says the LORD: About midnight I will go out through Egypt. ⁵Every firstborn in the land of Egypt shall die, from the firstborn of Pharaoh who sits on his throne to the firstborn of the female slave who is behind the handmill, and all the firstborn of the livestock. ⁶Then there will be a loud cry throughout the whole land of Egypt, such as has never been or will ever be again. ⁷But not a dog shall growl at any of the Israelites—not at people, not at animals—so that you may know that the LORD makes a distinction between Egypt and Israel. ⁸Then all these officials of yours shall come down to me, and bow low to me, saying, 'Leave us, you and all the people who follow you.' After that I will leave." And in hot anger he left Pharaoh.

We are living in a health crisis. A global pandemic, as declared by the World Health Organization. Coronavirus, now known as COVID-19, has turned the world on its head in the two months. During late-March/early-April, the entire country of Italy is shutdown. Fatalities across the US continue to rise. Politicians and scientists alike don't know what to do to stop the whole thing. Coronavirus has closed businesses, schools, and churches alike. The entire Las Vegas strip is deserted. Media outlets are releasing the latest numbers of infections and death by the minute. The president is spreading xenophobia through his reckless tweets. Hospitals are overrun, as first responders and social service workers remain on the front lines to offer services to all of us, and we continue to struggle with how to service the most vulnerable—the homeless, the elderly, and those in prison. Until early April, I continued to work in my field placement because children and youth alike still need guidance and support in this hour. The fight for social justice continues as organizations and politicians organize for low-wage workers and small businesses that are impacted by all this chaos. Even receiving a stimulus check for many people is the difference between food and no food. On Facebook, everyone is posting their opinion. Some people are saying that coronavirus is the beginning of the apocalypse. Others say it is no big deal. Some states are beginning to reopen, under great scrutiny that we are returning to "life as normal" way too soon. People continue to stock up on toilet paper at record highs. Naturopaths encourage the use of vitamins and herbal remedies to boost the immune systems. Debates spur about vaccination and inoculation. Some are blaming the widespread condition on the government because they did not heed the CDC's warnings sooner. People are sharing new articles every minute about the latest update. Social media influencers and entertainers are creating memes and videos while quarantined, with and without humor. The stock market is crashing and was bailed out every day during one week in March. Even the physical trading floor was closed for fear of spreading the virus. People who are infected and their families are speaking out about how it really feels to live in the middle of a situation for which you have no solution. One of my mom's friends said that she did not even know her cousin was sick with coronavirus and her family thought it was just a bad respiratory infection due to her asthma. Unfortunately, her cousin passed, and soon thereafter, her cousin's sister passed away, as well. People are living in chaos because it really feels like nobody can get a handle on what is going on. Is the virus ever going to stop spreading? Will it slow down? Will the quarantine work? Will a vaccine be discovered? Will it just dissipate like the other health epidemics we've had? What does tomorrow bring regarding coronavirus? A Christian might ask questions like will God heal our world? If so, when? Is God speaking to us through destruction? Is God's voice the same as it was in the book of Exodus, which was where we first canonically learned of plagues across the land? What is God saying and giving to believers who are living in these chaotic times?

God is saying that in these chaotic times, peace is available to us. Global pandemics, or plagues, are not new to the 21st century. Although we have a new health crisis every year, health crises have occurred throughout time. In the book of Exodus, God released a series of plagues on the land of Egypt because of Pharaoh's hard heart.[27] Although the plagues were a sign to Pharaoh, they impacted all people throughout the land. In a time of occupation and tension, plagues could have added an extra level of stress to the daily lives of the Israelites. As the plagues continued, God decided to show his people mercy through protection from the

27 Exodus 7–11.

final plague. Amid the chaos of the times, God gave peace and protection to the Israelites by making their hearts calm and by giving their firstborn sons protection from the Death Angel. This same peace and protection are available to all believers today. God's voice is still speaking to us loudly during our circumstances. God has not turned a deaf ear to our pains in this hour. Instead, God's covering of peace continues to be our shelter in this time of storm. Amid crisis, God promises peace to God's chosen people.

How do we experience God's peace in these chaotic times? In chaotic times, God's peace is evident through our trust in God's plan, God's protection over our lives, and our confidence in God's promises. God gives us peace by telling us that we can trust God with our future. God gives us peace by telling us that we are protected from the destruction of the future. God gives us peace by giving us confidence to boldly proclaim our victory. Having peace is the ability to have sanity and stability in chaos. Peace in thought, word, and deed allow us to reflect on our circumstances, instead of reacting to them. Peace gives us stillness and calmness when destruction and death are present. Peace during our circumstances anchors our faith in God, proving God does not leave us helpless. Peace is one of God's expressions of love towards believers.

Exodus 11:4–8 shows us how God intervened in the circumstance of the Israelites to give them peace amidst the plagues. The Israelites, like the Egyptians, also suffered from the plagues. They too were impacted by blood in their water, boils on their bodies, locusts, gnats, frogs, and the death of their livestock. As the last plague approached, all the people were physically, mentally, and emotionally drained from the devastation around them. However, during chaos, and with more plagues to come, God promised the Israelites that during the last plague, they would have stillness. This stillness came by way of God's protection from the Death Angel, and God's promise to God's people. The Israelites were able to activate their peace in God during this time first because Moses trusted the report that God gave him. The scripture foretold of the manifestation of God and the Israelites believed that would come to pass. Moses trusted that the plan God had for God's people would come to fruition. Likewise, we must trust the report of God in this moment. We can trust that God will bring us to a safe end. Like the Israelites, though, we cannot see the end of the road. Although scientists and statisticians are working tirelessly to get rid of coronavirus, the truth is that none of us really know when this will end and all of us will be impacted for a lifetime. However, we must trust whatever report God has for us in this hour. The report of God is where our trust should be, not the report of man. What if Moses trusted and believed Pharaoh's proclamation of Moses' testimony? If he had, Moses possibly would not be standing before Pharaoh in this moment. However, Moses trusted the report from God about his hopeful end. Moses was able to trust God because God told Moses that all would be well with him. The calmness and stillness of knowing that even after living through all the plagues, God's plan for protection would come for the people gave Moses an assurance in his faith. This is what we as believers should do as well. We should trust that God has a plan for our future, as Jeremiah says, to give us hope and an expected end.[28]

God's peace is also available through the many ways that God protects us in our hours of pestilence. As the final plague entered the land of Egypt, the Israelites were promised protection from it. The scripture says that there would be so much peace, not even a dog's bark would be heard.[29] This means that God was going to protect them from whatever was to come, leaving them unimpacted. As we find out, the Israelites had to take action to receive the protection; however, the protection was available to them. Likewise, protection is available to us. This passage in Exodus reminds us that even when there is destruction, chaos, turmoil, inequitable treatment, and even death, God is still present and still willing to lay God's hand of protection over God's people. Whereas our manifested protections are our masks, gloves, social distancing, and staying at home, we ultimately receive our protection from God. In taking the necessary precautions, we must credit God for protecting us from infection and/or death.

God's peace is given to us through our confidence in speech about our deliverance. In verse 8, Moses is audibly disgusted with Pharaoh's lack of belief. However, Pharaoh's dismissal only sparked Moses' intense confidence in God. Moses' declaration for the Israelites spoke firmly to the heart of Pharaoh. There was no quiver in speech or intent and through his speech impediment, Moses fiercely declared God's promises. In this moment, we must also fiercely declare our wellness, our family's wellness, and our world's wellness. Like the Israelites, we are still living in a plague, but our spirit of confidence and our speech of confidence will anchor our peace in God. In this hour, we cannot be double-tongued over ourselves because our energy will attract double-tongued results. We must stand confidently in God, like Moses did, that we will make it through this time.

God's presence and peace was promised to the Israelites before this moment in their history, just as God's presence and peace in our lives was promised to us before this moment in our history. Our response to the chaos of coronavirus will be indicative of who we trust and will reflect our belief in God's promises. Our response to the chaos around us is also indicative of to whom we belong. In the passage of Exodus, the scripture says, "...Then you will know that the Lord makes a distinction between the Egyptians and the Israelites."[30] This means that if we are God's people, our response to our circumstances should be different than those of the world. When the world is chaotic, we should be calm. When the

---

28 Jeremiah 29:11.
29 Exodus 11:7.
30 Exodus 11:7.

world is frantic, we should be still. When the world is believing man's report, we should be believing God's report of wellness and prosperity.

The events of the last plague had not yet occurred, so Moses had to trust God's plan. In this world crisis, we must trust that God will protect us so that we have peace despite our global situation. God's peace will calm our wandering minds, which are fueled by mass media, social media, death tolls, and the increasing pressures of opening or keeping our cities closed. Moment by moment, in an ever-changing world, it is easy to be swayed by every report. However, like Moses, in this hour, our response should be to heed the promises of God, which gives us assurance, protection, and peace.

Surviving Quarantine: Exodus 12:13, 22–23; Ephesians 3:16–19 (NIV)

JAMAR BOYD II

March 29, 2020

Exodus 12:13, 22–23

13 The blood will be a sign for you on the houses where you are, and when I see the blood, I will pass over you. No destructive plague will touch you when I strike Egypt. 22 Take a bunch of hyssop, dip it into the blood in the basin and put some of the blood on the top and on both sides of the doorframe. None of you shall go out of the door of your house until morning.

23 When the LORD goes through the land to strike down the Egyptians, he will see the blood on the top and sides of the doorframe and will pass over that doorway, and he will not permit the destroyer to enter your houses and strike you down.

Ephesians 3:16–19 (NIV)

16 I pray that out of his glorious riches he may strengthen you with power through his Spirit in your inner being, 17 so that Christ may dwell in your hearts through faith. And I pray that you, being rooted and established in love, 18 may have power, together with all the Lord's holy people, to grasp how wide and long and high and deep is the love of Christ, 19 and to know this love that surpasses knowledge—that you may be filled to the measure of all the fullness of God.

Words have seemingly been inadequate to describe the state of our current dilemma in America, and across the world. One virus, COVID-19 (coronavirus), has literally gripped the world and caused all of humanity to cease. The United States now tops the globe with known cases, exceeding 100,000, and 1,000+ deaths. These statistics coupled with uncertainty among families and communities, only worsens with inconsistent guidelines from the federal government and states adding to human fear and concern. It's in moments like this when our minds begin to consider inconceivable possibilities and outcomes, all the while remaining hopeful and optimistic of the days ahead. Because the reality is, while this strand of coronavirus is unknown, causing us to adjust our lives, it's not the first time we've faced a crisis nor been admonished to quarantine.

The pandemic of 1918 is noted as the deadliest health pandemic in history. And like today schools, churches, nonessential business, and places of entertainment were closed. Funerals were restricted to graveside services; usual or large gatherings were prohibited as families were urged to commune together in their houses and pray for relief. We can all recall moments in life where we've battled an illness and were given the instructions to, "stay inside and sweat it out." Others can think back to times when our parent or guardian instructed us to "stay inside, it's too dangerous out there right now." The concept, exercising, and needed time of temporary social distancing isn't new. Quarantine stretches back even further in history.

The twelfth chapter of Exodus is an introductory course on surviving quarantine. God gives Moses clear instructions to relay to the people of Israel amid the time known as 'Passover.' The Lord tells Moses, "each household is to obtain a lamb on the 10th day of the month, kill the lamb at twilight on the 14th day, take some of the blood and put it on two doorposts and lintel of the house where they'll feast, eat, and await the Passover. At that time, I the Lord, will see the blood and pass over you, and no plague will befall you to destroy you."[31] With these very instructions Moses returns to the people and in verses 21–23, he instructs them on how to survive quarantine. Admonishing them to, "Take a bunch of hyssop and dip it in the blood that is in the basin and touch the lintel and the two doorposts with the blood that is in the basin. None of you shall go out of the door of his house until the morning. For the Lord will pass through to strike the Egyptians, and when he sees the blood on the lintel and on the two doorposts, the Lord will pass over the door and will not allow the destroyer to enter your houses to strike you." Like the children of Israel, we are merely trying to survive amid a global health pandemic. No, we don't have to kill a lamb and place blood on our doorposts for Jesus Christ has shed his blood for us, which is still at work in the earth. Yet, quarantine is at hand. What do we do when Passover seemingly re-emerges in 2020? What do we do when social distancing is ordered to survive the "time at hand"?

31 Exodus 12:1–3.

We must: 1. Apply the Solution; 2. Adhere to the Command; and 3. Await the Relief.

APPLY THE SOLUTION

Within Moses's instructions to the people of Israel they were admonished to apply a solution, the lamb's blood by way of dipping the hyssop branches into it and covering the doorpost. Utilizing hyssop was not strange to the people as the plant was used in rituals for ceremonial cleansing and atonement. Within an hour of crisis and survival, they were not told to utilize some strange ointment, concoction, or sab but that which was common to them – lamb's blood (as done by the priest for the cleansing of sin and hyssop, that the blood applied may cover the doorframe). It says something that in a moment of angst and uncertainty, God did not command them to derive a new solution but to adequately apply that already in place to cleanse and protect. Sometimes the wheel doesn't have to be reinvented, we just have to use what's before us.

The Center for Disease Control and healthcare professionals have reiterated consistently, that proper cleansing of one's hands (frequently) and sanitization (of your environment and living quarters) are the best means of protection amid this outbreak. Instantaneously thousands flocked to convenience and grocery stores to purchase hand sanitizer, soap, gloves, and masks to protect themselves from COVID-19. No stone was left unturned as aisles were quickly emptied of these seemingly rarely used items, turned essential.

City and state governments found the time to clean, sanitize, and refurbish otherwise ignored areas of human interactions such as bus stops, train station tracks and entrances to name a few. Without hesitation citizens relied on solutions already encouraged for daily use, to survive.

Growing up my mother, inclusive of my grandparents, always commanded us to wash our hands the moment we came in the house from outside, place our dirty clothes in the hamper so they could be readily washed, hop in the shower, and cleanse our bodies thoroughly. This meant using enough soap to cover the totality of our doorposts aka our bodies to rid of the germs, funk, and unsanitary matters we brought into the house. The commonality in all this is, we must apply the solution that is already before us. Soap and water, hand sanitizer, strong cleaning products, and the more have seemingly been mainstays in black households; yet more now than ever the consistent need to apply the solutions properly is elevated.

The children of Israel understood the significance of the blood, the solution, for atonement and sacrificial purposes just as we understand the power of Jesus's blood for our redemption, at work even in this hour. Child of God, applying the solution is just one step to surviving quarantine next we must adhere to the command.

ADHERE TO THE COMMAND

Drs. Birx and Fauci have given instructions to the American people on how to properly sanitize, social distance, and quarantine amid this virus. Daily news briefings are held to enlighten the public of pandemic updates, yet the attention is truly fixated on these two esteemed medical professionals especially Dr. Fauci. We've been told to stay at least 6ft. from another individual, omit attending large gatherings—no more than 10 people, and more importantly quarantine; only leaving our homes for essential needs. These are the commands to which we must adhere. Yet, it's not easy.

Living in a culture, society, and world where human interaction is the exchange being confined to one's home willingly is not easy. No longer is it good for the survival of humanity to host large gatherings, attend a dinner party, visit relatives, or even attend church because you could place someone's health at risk unknowingly. That's the crazy thing about this virus. Its symptoms are eerily like the flu, one may lose sensory abilities like taste and smell, a lite cough can intensify rapidly, and those with compromised immune systems, preexisting conditions, and/or over 60 are the most vulnerable. Therefore, for the good of humanity we must adhere to the commands of social distancing and quarantine.

I began to reflect upon the complexity of social seclusion and separation within our national and global context. We exist in a world where trade is a daily activity. We exchange goods whether it be conversation, business deals, emotional and verbal encouragement, physical presence, or just merely supporting a friend or neighbor at life's difficult moments. I began to dig deeper into the harshness of isolation for those who are already imprisoned, hospitalized, confined to a nursing or rehab facility where visitation is already limited or prohibited.

I really sat in the possible agony of enduring this alone while battling anxiety, depression, substance abuse, grief, or the inability to just fight. Truly, my mind kept going and stepped onto the banks of the shore of those who are high school seniors, others in the final phase of their undergraduate or, like me, graduate studies who won't have a commencement ceremony, some who had recently applied for jobs or accepted an offer that may not exist any longer, scores of those who are now laid off or unemployed, and the millions uncertain about tomorrow. And I could not escape considering the families of those infected and dying across the world. All of this is real and cannot be escaped or removed but must be endured amid quarantine. Therefore, the question is raised, "how do we interact and survive amid this crisis?"

Moses in verse 22 had given them the solution, but in the "b" clause he enforces the command. He tells them, "None of you shall go out of the door of your house until morning." A clear indication of social distancing and quarantine for the children of Israel. States and cities across the country have instituted stay at home orders for the safety of residents. Schools across the country are closed and college/universities have resorted to online learning to complete the semester. Businesses and companies have been forced to cease daily operations, with employees working from home, and delivery or take out as the only means of consumer exchange. Our daily lives and the world large are adjusting to the command at hand. Therefore, quality time with family, rest from the hustle, and separation from normalcy have commenced.

Surviving this looks different for everyone, yet we're all in this together. Neighbors have pitched in to ensure families and seniors have groceries. Local governments are taking necessary measures to prohibit the taxation of residents amid economic uncertainty; churches have adopted, created, and/or utilized creative technological mediums to interact with their congregations to ensure hope and ministry continues; teachers and students now interact through Zoom, facetime, conference call, and other methods to ensure learning continues; and families draw closer during this hour through conversation, Instagram challenges, and TikTok dances. While all are not adhering to the command to quarantine, there's a noticeable commitment to survive this thing together. Leaving nothing left to do but await the relief.

AWAIT THE RELIEF

The children of Israel understood if we apply the solution and adhere to the command, our relief is sure to come. Within the 23rd they are told, "and when he sees the blood on the lintel and on the two doorposts, the Lord will pass over the door and will not allow the destroyer to enter your houses to strike you." Seemingly a cause and effect exchange. Follow the prior steps and relief, a stimulus, will surely be your portion. Contextually we understand their condition, historically we acknowledge their reality and the practices already in place, and through faith we too believe that relief is coming.

The United States Congress on Friday, March 27th passed the largest economic stimulus bill in American history, topping $2 trillion dollars.[32] Senate Republicans and Democrats engaged a long debate arguing over what was valid

---

32 Jacob Pramuk. "Senate Passes $2 Trillion Coronavirus Relief Bill—House Aims for Friday Vote," *CNBC*. March 25, 2020. https://www.cnbc.com/2020/03/25/senate-passes-2-trillion-coronavirus-stimulus-package.html

and invalid, regarding meeting the needs of the people. Some stood on the side of fiscal conservatism, others balanced the scale, while many argued that there is no number too big to save lives and supply the people with financial resources. When the bill financially reached the House of Representatives lawmakers stated their claims, yet the words of Rep. Ayanna Pressley, days before the vote struck a chord with me, "If it's a radical notion that people's lives are more important than corporate bailouts, call me radical."[33] Oh, what poignancy.

Regardless of political affiliation most citizens have been fixated on the 24-hour news coverage of this virus, just trying to see when relief will come. They've heard the pleas of nurses and doctors. They've seen images from hospitals around the country and world. Observed the total contracted count juxtaposed with the mortality stats. The signing of this bill led many to rejoice, because a check will be coming in the mail. Yet, there are some fine details that impact our lives and prayerfully will be resolved in a manner of equity and justice. Nevertheless, the words of Rep. Pressley still ring loud in my ear as the hope of Jesus Christ resonates in my soul; "If it's a radical notion that people's lives are more important than corporate bailouts, call me radical."

Child of God, that's faith actualized, embodied, and enacted. The work and life of Jesus Christ reveals unto us that life is so much more important than corporate greed and governmental destruction of human morale and longevity. That's the radical nature of Jesus's blood which covers our doorposts making us one body amid calamity, with the assurance that the Holy Spirit will enable, keep, and strengthen us. Therefore, enabling me to take the words of Paul in Ephesians 3:16–19 sharing in this great hope, "I pray that out of his glorious riches he may strengthen you with power through his Spirit in your inner being, so that Christ may dwell in your hearts through faith. And I pray that you, being rooted and established in love, may have power, together with all the Lord's holy people, to grasp how wide and long and high and deep is the love of Christ, and to know this love that surpasses knowledge—that you may be filled to the measure of all the fullness of God." Even in this hour of uncertainty and ever-changing reports, may you be rooted in the presence of Christ within you. Knowing that the Holy Spirit will strengthen and keep us forever, enabling us to delve deeper in God's love, and stand evermore upon the glory of Christ Jesus. A love that is boundless, beyond human comprehension, full of God's sovereign grace and mercy that we may obtain the glorious and miraculous relief.

So, "Now to him who is able to do immeasurably more than all we ask or imagine, according to his power that is at work within us, to him be glory in the church and in Christ Jesus throughout all generations, for ever and ever! Amen."[34]

---

33 Ayanna Pressley, *Twitter*, March 24, 2020. https://twitter.com/ayannapressley/status/1242610930757898244
34 Ephesians 3:20–21.

Hope in the Holla: Numbers 27:1-5 (NRSV)

DONNA VANHOOK

June 28, 2020

[1]Then the daughters of Zelophehad came forward. Zelophehad was son of Hepher son of Gilead son of Machir son of Manasseh son of Joseph, a member of the Manassite clans. The names of his daughters were: Mahlah, Noah, Hoglah, Milkah, and Tirzah. [2]They stood before Moses, Eleazar the priest, the leaders, and the congregation, at the entrance of the tent of meeting, and they said, [3]"Our father died in the wilderness; he was not among the company of those who gathered themselves together against the LORD in the company of Korah, but died for his own sin; and he had no sons. [4]Why should the name of our father be taken away from his clan because he had no son? Give to us a possession among our father's brothers." [5]Moses brought their case before the LORD.

Beloved of God, halfway through the year 2020, we find ourselves in the midst of a global coronavirus pandemic that disproportionately affects black communities. Unfortunately, only the coronavirus is the current pandemic accepted as a public health crisis. Black men and Black women frequently die at the hands of badge wearing, gun toting persons sworn to protect and to serve. While COVID-19 seemingly shut down global travel, slowing down production of goods essential for living, there has been an ongoing pandemic for centuries that may hopefully be declared a public health crisis in a way Charlotte, North Carolina, at least acknowledges the need to do so for racial justice.

You see, civilian cell phone and law enforcement videos constantly show some form of abuse of power or authority against black bodies. Not many days pass until the world witnesses, once again, white women and men making frivolous or false claims against black folks doing everyday activities.[35] Those guardians of invisible white space appear to take upon themselves the responsibility to call police departments to keep black bodies from infiltrating imaginary boundaries of whiteness. The calls for re-enforcement endanger the lives of black women, men, girls, and boys. Countless numbers of whom are gunned down in the public sphere like Rayshard Brooks was killed in a Wendy's parking lot. Many were at home minding their own business—#SayHerName, Atatiana Jefferson killed at home when playing video games with her nephew. Some were even trying to rest in bed—#SayHerName, Breonna Taylor killed when police tried to serve a no-knock warrant at the wrong address.

Lethal force seems to have taken a turn for the worse with senseless murders of black bodies by police officers. Can we admit the likelihood of trauma from watching the numerous recordings of police officers, in these yet to be united states, unjustifiably shooting unarmed black women, men, girls and boys as though they were big game in the wilderness? All 50 states of the union have erupted in protest; Amish communities are standing in the streets holding signs, and country after country stands in solidarity with Black America. My friends, All Black Lives Matter. #HonkIfYouHearMe!

The racism embedded in every system has historically led to scrutiny of this nation's policing practices against black bodies. Maybe racism will be broadly designated as a public health crisis. What else must it take? Visible to the whole world was a white male police officer pressing his weight into a kneeling position on a handcuffed black man face down on the pavement. The officer held the position for nearly nine minutes (8 minutes and 46 seconds) on cell phone video while George Floyd hollered in pain, "I Can't Breathe." Floyd, no doubt, losing consciousness, called out to his deceased mother for help.

The world responded to Floyd's holler with demands for police reform, calling for tougher consequences in excessive uses of lethal force, namely against unarmed black persons. From its beginning in this country, policing was established as a method to keep the enslaved bound by the will of their enslavers. Being counted as only 3/5 human, chattel, property of the highest bidder, the enslaved endured white supremacy in policing by way of slave patrols. In times past, White persons were equipped with the law, slave codes, and whatever means necessary to keep enslaved Africans in their place.

---

35 Amir Vera and Laura Ly, "White woman who called police on black man bird-watching in Central Park has been fired," *CNN*, May 26, 2020, https://www.cnn.com/2020/05/26/us/cent ral-park-video-dog-video-african-american-trnd/index.html

I am reminded of reading in the spiritual autobiography of one of the first black female preachers, *Memoir of Old Elizabeth, a Coloured Woman*, an encounter of a similar slave patrol during the time she started itinerary preaching, in 1808. She told the story of a "watchman" entered sacred space while she was on a journey doing ministry in the home where women had gathered to hear the word of God. The women were afraid. Most left, however, Elizabeth stayed and boldly made the sacrifice to speak her truth to the watchman who stated he was there to "break up your meeting." She stood her ground, not wavering in faith, shared the gospel with him, laid hands on him; then the watchman humbly left the house with an apology to the few women who remained, allowing them to continue the service uninterrupted.

Here you need to know, in the year 1766, Old Elizabeth was born in Maryland. She majestically encountered God at the age of twelve after defiantly leaving a slave farm to find her mother. She risked being beaten in order to connect with the woman who bore her. After spending time bonding, her mother told Elizabeth, "she had nobody in the world to look to but God"[36] then sent her back to the plantation where the overseer severely whipped her.

To this A. Elaine Brown Crawford writes in *Hope in the Holler: A Womanist Theology*:

> The abuses of slavery made it poignantly clear that there was no one to rely on but Jesus and God. The religion of America denied Old Elizabeth unhindered worship in the church, but the religion of Jesus enabled her to 'have church' wherever she was...Her spirit was taught how to pray, "'Lord, have mercy on me—Christ save me.'" [The Holy Spirit] told her "all the hope she had of being saved was no more than a (single strand of hair), still pray, and it would be sufficient"... Old Elizabeth embodied the religion of Jesus and the hope of female slaves.[37]

Brown Crawford goes on, "Slave women did not just talk about the possibilities for their lives and communities—they pursued the possibilities. Their theology lived through them...The passion for freedom, humanity and voice emboldened slave women to take extraordinary, radical means to achieve personal and communal liberation."[38]

So now, during this preaching moment, I want to unfold for you a story about five extraordinary biological sisters in the Book of Numbers, chapter 27, who set precedence for future generations of women. You need to know Mahlah, Noah, Hoglah, Milkah and Tirzah, say their names, were unmarried daughters of Zelophehad, whose name means protection from fear. Their parents had died

---

36   Elizabeth, Memoir of Old Elizabeth, A Coloured Woman (Philadelphia: Collins, 1863), 27.
37   A. Elaine Brown Crawford, *Hope in the Holler: A Womanist Theology* (Louisville: Westminster John Knox Press, 2002), 32.
38   Ibid., 40.

along with the generation of Israelites wandering in the wilderness of Sinai. Verse 1 explains how their genealogy connects with the twelve tribes of Israel through Joseph the dreamer, father of Manasseh and Ephraim.

We note here the relevance of the Book of Numbers to the Hebrew Bible. Numbers derives its name from the census counts. The census was taken in chapter one and then again in chapter 26 where in verse 33 it was discovered Zelophehad did not have any sons. These reports differ because of the actions of some of the Israelites between the chapters. They argued and complained throughout their time in the wilderness. In chapter 16, the Bible says the sons of Korah banded together against their leaders Moses and his brother Aaron, the High Priest.

So then, God intervened to disrupt the plans of unruly people who failed to join with the whole of the Israelite community preparing to occupy the New Canaan land. These folks were out of order, so to speak. They called themselves opposing Moses and Aaron but found themselves fighting against God. By chapter 26, with the exception of Moses, all of the generation of Israelites who crossed the Red Sea with him died out as a result of their consistent acting outside of God's will, including Moses' brother Aaron and sister Miriam the prophet. They were unwilling to follow simple rules or patiently wait on God's right time to possess land promised to them.

Now, the petition of bold and brilliant sisters in chapter 27 verses three and four makes more sense. The census had shown they were the only survivors of Zelophehad. In verse two they approach the entrance to the tent of meetings, the place where the leaders consulted among themselves before Moses spoke to God on behalf of the Israelite community. Mahlah, Noah, Hoglah, Milcah and Tirzah, #SayTheirNames, made their way through the crowd, close enough where Moses could hear them.

Consider the faith of these five sisters for a moment. In the absence of fear, they rolled up on Moses and the High Priest Eleazar in front of the rest of the Israelite community questioning Israelite law and the concept of primogeniture. Primogeniture means after the death of the father, inheritance of land and property belonged to the father's first-born son. The father, paterfamilias, during this time was head of the household. He normally bestowed upon the firstborn son all rights and privileges regardless of the number of other children. After the sons, from first to last, brothers of the father came next in line as heirs. The customs of that day recognized daughters, along with wives, as a part of the father's possessions until marriage. Thereafter, daughters belonged to their husband's family. Marriages were often prearranged so the daughters commonly had no voice in whose possession they may become.

For the most part, daughters at this time of antiquity were not counted among those who would receive an inheritance. That is with the exception of Zelophehad's daughters advocating for themselves here in Numbers 27. You know these were some bad sisters to envision speaking to Moses about their petition after a whole generation had been wiped out for speaking out of turn and behaving contrary to God's guidance through Moses and Aaron.

Womanist scholar Delores Williams wrote, unity among the sisters was a primary factor in their obtaining economic justice.[39] Both Moses and God advocated for the women when they petitioned for change. When they deliberated and decided to speak as a unified group with the hope of seeing their dilemma resolved, they found favor with humankind and with God. Let this be a lesson for us all. When we come together on one accord as a community of believers, anything is possible!

Now, I imagine at least one of Zelophehad's daughters had extraordinary sight of a visionary, a dreamer; she had big thoughts outside of the box. Maybe she put a buzz in one sister's ear and then called another to the side. It could have been the oldest, the middle or the baby sister. Regardless of who imparted the vision, at least one of them had the mind to see beyond their Israelite customs and matters of law during the era in which they lived. The sisters came together in strength and hope to speak something never before attempted. All they had was one another, God, Hope and a Holla. But guess what? That's all they needed.

As it was, the five sisters got Moses' attention, not concerned at the time about consequences. Can't you hear them Holla: Hey Moses listen, "Our father died in the desert. You know he was not among Korah's followers, who banded together against the Lord, but he died for his own sin and left no sons. Now tell us, why should our father's name disappear from his clan? Because he had no son?"

Moses took their bold statement before God in verse five. God replied in verses seven through eleven, Zelophehad's daughters were right in their petition for their father's inheritance of property, preserving *his* place in the lineage of Manasseh. God answered the sisters as they represented a new generation of women transformed by a new way of thinking and acting on faith. The sisters were shielded from fear as their father's name indicates and they had been born through the generations of a dreamer. Nothing seemed impossible for them.

Although God amended the law in chapter 36 to keep the land within the family clans, the names Mahlah, Noah, Hoglah, Milkah and Tirzah, #SayTheirNames, will always be remembered in Israelite history concerning the matter of inheritance for daughters and women's rights within their family. Keep in mind, traditionally, they had no leg to stand on but when God is for you who can be against you? God can change tradition; God can make provisions for changing policy. If you dare to plan and organize for change, God can make ways out of

---

39 Delores Williams, "A Theology of Advocacy for Women" *Church and Society* (Nov./ Dec. 2000), 5.

no way, so put it into action. With one Holla, case law was established for these young women giving us hope today that taking a stand can yield transformation.

You've heard it said, you can't fight city hall. Well, these sisters challenged the status quo. Together they knocked down barriers to their father's inheritance of land. Together they had hope in God change would come in their favor; for God alone had the power to change their situation. Yes, my friends, there *is* Hope in the Holla.

We now have hope in God for many reasons because when the world needed to be saved God provided the ultimate sacrifice for sin. The Bible says in Romans 8:24–25, "For in hope we were saved. Now hope that is seen is not hope. For who hopes for what is seen? But if we hope for what we do not see, we wait for it with patience."

I want to encourage everyone who hears this message to keep Hope alive! I want you to know "*My Hope* is built on nothing less than Jesus' blood and righteousness; I dare not trust the sweetest frame, But wholly lean on Jesus' name. On Christ the solid Rock I stand all other ground is sinking sand."[40] I tell you the truth, there's something about the name of Jesus. He's the one who has all powers in his hands. "That name, that name Jesus. Oh, how I love to call His name."[41] Jesus hears my cry, and He answers by and by. Every time I have needed Jesus, he has not let me down. "He's a battle axe in the time of battle, a shelter in the time of storm."[42]

Throughout U.S. history, wise black women have been speaking our Hope in God. It is no wonder Black women have historically put our hope in God to resist and defy racial oppression, browbeating and other assaults upon our black bodies by men who called themselves owning us. Yes, this hope has shown itself in our survival from the time our foremothers were first brought to this country over the middle passage throughout history to this year of COVID-19 and police brutality, in the year 2020.

When we have Hope in Jesus, we can speak things which are not as though they were. We have faith knowing troubles don't last always. We can speak to a mountain of trouble, if we believe and do not doubt, we can say to the mountain move and it will move from here to there.[43] All we need is the faith of a mustard seed, mountain moving faith to believe nothing is impossible with God.

40 African American Heritage Hymnal, "The Solid Rock" (Chicago, IL: GIA Publishing, 2001), 385.

41 The Rance Allen Group, "Something about the Name Jesus," 2004, The Live Experience, CD.

42 Clay Evans, "He's a Battle Axe" August 9, 2000, *Rev. Clay Evans Presents: The African American Religious Connection Mass Choir, He's a Battle-Axe*, CD.

43 Matthew 17:20, NRSV.

So, my sister and my brother, keep Hope Alive! Keep Hope Alive! Keep Hope Alive! There is Hope in your Holla!

The Ministry of Manna: Deuteronomy 8:1–5 (NRSV)

HOWARD-JOHN WESLEY

April 20, 2020

1 This entire commandment that I command you today you must diligently observe, so that you may live and increase, and go in and occupy the land that the Lord promised on oath to your ancestors. 2 Remember the long way that the Lord your God has led you these forty years in the wilderness, in order to humble you, testing you to know what was in your heart, whether or not you would keep his commandments. 3 He humbled you by letting you hunger, then by feeding you with manna, with which neither you nor your ancestors were acquainted, in order to make you understand that one does not live by bread alone, but by every word that comes from the mouth of the Lord. 4 The clothes on your back did not wear out and your feet did not swell these forty years. 5 Know then in your heart that as a parent disciplines a child so the Lord your God disciplines you.

Like all of us, I awaken each day of this pandemic trying to adjust to and accept the new realities of the world in which we live. It has not been easy. Practicing social distancing and remaining 6ft away from people. It's not been easy staying in the house while the sun is shining. It's not been easy celebrating the resurrection of Jesus at home for the first time in my entire life. It's not been easy making sure I have my mask when I go out to the store. People's patience has been shortened, I was at the store just yesterday and apparently, I got too close to a woman who told me, "I'm going need you to back up, you might have Rona." Every day looks the same and I wake up struggling to remember what day it is. It has not been easy.

Our struggle is not primarily physical, it is also mental and emotional, taking a deeper toll on us than we ever assumed. What's most unsettling for me is the uncertainty that surrounds us. We live in the midst of absolute uncertainty. Let me say that again, we live in the midst of absolute uncertainty.

In this midst of this pandemic, the only thing we do know, is what we don't know. Every day the data, the information, the numbers, the science, the time-lines, the severity of and about this virus are changing. We are fed lies from our President, mixed reporting on media, and all the while people are dying. All we know – is what we don't know. We don't know when a vaccine will be available. We don't know when PPE will be available for medical personnel. We don't know how to truly protect ourselves from contracting COVID-19. We don't know how long the virus lives on surfaces and in the air. We don't know how long we will be sheltered in our homes before it's safe to go out. We don't know when the schools will reopen or when we can come back to church. All we know is what we don't know. There's no information we can truly trust. No answers we can rest assured in. No hope of good news we can hang our hats on. All we know is what we don't know.

If the truth be told, uncertainty is unsettling for a several reasons. It reminds us that we can't control everything, science doesn't have every answer, human hands can't fix everything and even at our best we can't predict or handle all that life will bring our way. We can try to use every resource at our disposal to make certain that life follows the course we've charted and plays out the way we dreamed, and things go down in ways we can handle. But sometimes all we know is what we don't know, and uncertainty abounds. Uncertainty is fertile soil for fear, anxiety, worry, stress, depression, and even doubts about God, and God's goodness, God's care.

And that's not just in this pandemic, that's in life. Life has a way of delivering us into seasons where we have more questions than answers, no clue of what's really going, no sense of when things will get better, no assurances that we trust fully, no timelines, no vaccines, no new offers and opportunities, and days when today looks just like yesterday and tomorrow will be a repeat of today.

That's where the people of God are for forty years of their journey, as they wander in the wilderness without any clue of where they are going and when the wilderness would end. The bulk of first five books of the Bible is a story of wandering in the wilderness. No one could have ever predicted that the joy of crossing the Red Sea would be followed by forty years of wandering. They never knew they would land in places where there was no food and no water. They didn't know they would see so many loved ones die on the way. I doubt they would have followed Moses out of Egypt if they knew what he truly didn't know. They didn't know they would have to walk where they had never walked before headed someplace none of them had even seen, trusting God like before. They didn't know their faith would be tested like it would and there would be days where they had no idea of where they were going or when they would get there.

The wilderness is a place of uncertainty and uncertainty is the wilderness of life. Wilderness is when you didn't see it coming and weren't prepared for it. Wilderness is when you have no clue when it will end. Wilderness is when you feel there is no one you call on or trust in. Wilderness is when there are no assurances or answers. Wilderness is living through situations that you never dealt with before. Wilderness is when resources are running low. Wilderness is when you ask every day, when will life get back to some kind of normal?

But here's what they found out, that I share with you in our wilderness of uncertainty, God was with them, and God is with us. God was guiding them through their uncertainties. One of the primary assurances of God's presence in the wilderness was manna.

Read fully about manna when it first appears in Exodus 16. Manna was bread that would fall at night like dew and the children of Israel would collect it in the morning and that was their daily diet for forty years.

The interesting thing about Manna is that the term *manna* does not translate as bread. In Hebrew, manna is not even a noun. Manna is a question, *what is it?* Manna literally means, what is this? When they saw it, they didn't know what it was because they had never seen it before. They didn't know how it got there, they didn't know what it would taste like, they didn't know if they would enjoy it. It was a surprise to them every morning. As former slaves they understood crops and harvest, they knew about sowing and reaping, they knew what it was to live off the fruit of their own labor but never had they experienced something just showing up out of nowhere.

What's curious to me is that they continued to call it manna even after they had tasted it. They never called it bread or heavenly bread or food or some other title. They labeled it as a question that they had eat every day. Every morning, for forty years, they awakened and said "manna," what is this? They raised that question every day. Maybe one of the reasons they never renamed it as bread is because in the wilderness you have to learn to live with questions that may have no answers. There will be seasons of life when what you go through leaves you waking up every day with a questions. Questions like why God? When Lord? How could you Jesus? What did I do God? Why did she have to die? Why was I laid off? How could this happen to us? Where were you when I needed you most? Have you ever lived in a season on questions? If you have then you know manna.

The tough part is that the answer to the question is not really an answer. When the children of Israel raised the question, the only answer Moses could give was "God provides." The answer to their question was not an answer but rather an assurance; the assurance, *God provides.*

That's a word because as a child of God there will be some wilderness moment when we live with the tension and uncertainty of questions that may never be answered. You may never know why it went down the way it did. You may never understand why God allowed that to happen. You may never fully figure it out or get an answer that puts it to rest. But in that moment, allow me to play Moses in your life and give you the same assurance, *God provides*.

I believe in every wilderness moment of your life when you're questioning God, God is questioning you in return. Do you trust me? Do you trust every promised I've made to you? Do you trust that I will never leave nor forsake you? Do you trust that all things will work together for your good? Do you trust that this weeping will only last for a night? Do you trust God?

While you're debating your answer to that question allow me to remind you of how many manna moments you've already had in life and how many times the Lord has provided. How many times has the Lord provided, made a way, sent a blessing, opened a door, moved a mountain, held back the enemy, delivered from a situation. If you have ever experienced the Lord providing, if you've ever been blessed in a way you know you can't take credit for, if you've ever seen the Lord show up and make a way then you know manna and you know God provides.

Here's what's interesting about manna, this wilderness provision, there were some specific instructions God gave the children of Israel about manna. Some instructions that will prove helpful for anyone in a season of uncertainty. Can I share a few with you today?

God gave specific instructions on gathering manna. In Exodus 16, they were told to gather it first thing in the morning because by mid-morning it would be gone. It would evaporate and disappear when the sun started to rise. Don't miss this. God says, "I'm going to provide for you in the wilderness but the first thing you have to do in the morning is identify and lay hands on what I've provided."

That's a word. When you're wandering in the wilderness, and living with uncertainty, what you do first thing in the morning is critical for the rest of your day. God declares that before you check your phone to see what text messages you missed, before you get on social media to see who said what, before you turn on CNN to hear data about virus, take a moment to identify the provisions and the blessings that the Lord has given you already. Before you get out the bed, before you wipe the sleep out of your eye, before you brush away your morning breath, pause and name what the Lord has provided and thank God for your manna. Thank God for your eyes opening. Thank God for your spouse and children. Thank God for the clothes in the closet. Thank God for a roof over head. Thank God for heat in your home. Thank God for your manna.

May I suggest to you that the wilderness is a place of renewed appreciation and thanksgiving for what we too often take for granted.

If I know people, like I know people, there were somebodies who saw the manna and weren't initially grateful. They were somebodies who compared it to the onions of Egypt and said "I'm not eating that." There were somebodies who saw it on the ground and said, "that's nasty." There were somebodies who saw how it looked and said, "I deserve more than this." There are always somebodies who fail to appreciate what the Lord has done. Look at somebody at tell them, "I hope he's not talking about you?" Are you that somebody that has failed to be grateful?

So, watch this, God takes away everything they were used to eating and provides them with nothing but manna for forty years. How long can you eat the same thing before you get sick of it? How many days can you eat leftovers before you don't want it anymore. In the wilderness we are challenged to see what the Lord has provided and ask ourselves this question: am I sick of it or am I thankful for it? Am I sick of being at home or am I thankful that I have a home? Am I sick of the online schooling for my kids or am I thankful for the time I can spend with them? Am I sick of working from home or am I grateful that I still have a job?

In the wilderness God teaches us not to take for granted what we should be grateful for. And maybe, just maybe, that's one good take away from this pandemic – a renewed appreciation and thanksgiving for the Lord has been providing. The wilderness opens your eyes to what God has blessed you with and teaches you to be thankful. Is there anyone here who's grateful for some things you used to take for granted?

Not only did they have to gather it early in the morning, but they could only gather but so much. They could only gather as much as they needed, not as much as they wanted but as much as each household needed. Now, watch what happened. Some people tried to gather more than they needed because they were greedy, and it meant that others weren't able to get enough to meet their need. The greed of some infringed on the need of others. So, the Lord engaged in a little Christian socialism and distributed the manna evenly so that everyone had what they needed.

In the wilderness God forces us to examine the difference between our need and our greed, learning the difference between what we want and what we truly need. This is a good lesson for a consumer capitalist Christianity that peddled prophetic prosperity and profit and injected greed into the gospel. We have reached a wilderness place of self-examination where we must ask, how much is enough? How many cars do we need? How many shoes can we wear? Do I need a new outfit for every event? Am I spending more on myself than I am giving to those in need? Does my greed prevent me from helping meet someone else's need?

I feel compelled to remind us in this pandemic wilderness that if you're blessed to have excess you also have an obligation to help those with less. It's a shame for those living in excess with things they cannot use to be next to those who are hungry, naked, homeless, and without basic needs.

They could only gather it one day at a time, they could only gather as much as they needed but finally it could not be kept overnight except on the Sabbath. In the wilderness the Lord was teaching his people to live one day at a time. Sometimes you enter a season of life where your deepest concern is not tomorrow, not next month or next year but rather this day. That is not to say that we shouldn't make plans, or create vision boards, or engage in strategic planning but rather that we should not be anxious or fearful about tomorrow.

This is what Jesus pressed upon us when he taught us to pray, "give us *this day our daily bread.*" This is what he meant when he taught us in Matthew 6 to not be so anxious about tomorrow that we miss today. Jesus reminds us that if God can feed the birds, if God cares enough about the grass, then surely God will take care of us. So, don't live your life in worry, make a deliberate decision to trust God today and believe that God will take care of tomorrow.

My oldest son has just began learning how to drive. Even though it's been a pleasant experience teaching him to drive, it has also been nerve wrecking at times. At times I found myself pumping my imaginary break on the passenger side or grabbing on my seatbelt for dear life as he got too close to another car or the curb. But every day he's been getting better and I've been relaxing more and more so much so that I even fell asleep in the car with him the other day. He's proven himself one day at a time and I've learned to trust him. He's handled situations one day at a time and I've learned to trust him. He's gotten us home safely one day at a time and I've learned to trust him. And that, beloved, is one of the final lessons of manna – learning to trust God one day at a time. He's proven himself; he's handled situations, he's gotten you home time and time again so trust God to provide. The song writer put it best...

> Be not dismayed whatever betide
> God will take care of you.
> Beneath his wings of love abide
> God will take care of you.[44]

---

44 Traditional gospel hymn, "God Will Take Care of You".

What Does All this Mean?: Joshua 4:5-7 (NIV)

WALLIS C. BAXTER III

May 24, 2020

5 and said to them, "Go over before the ark of the LORD your God into the middle of the Jordan. Each of you is to take up a stone on his shoulder, according to the number of the tribes of the Israelites, 6 to serve as a sign among you. In the future, when your children ask you, 'What do these stones mean?' 7 tell them that the flow of the Jordan was cut off before the ark of the covenant of the LORD. When it crossed the Jordan, the waters of the Jordan were cut off. These stones are to be a memorial to the people of Israel forever."

Here we are in month three of the widespread awareness of COVID-19. The reality is that we've been in this space for quite some time. Oh, we've only been in quarantine for a few months, but those of us who have been kissed by the sun, of the darker hue, black and brown in America, we've been here for quite a while. Truth be told, we came here in quarantine. Truth be told, those who originated in this country, the Native Americans, have been in quarantine since the first "discoverers" landed on this country's eastern shores. Truth be told, there are brown individuals and families from beyond our southern borders who have been in quarantine. These truths have plagued this nation since its inception. This inability, it seems, is for the dominant and dominating culture to live up to and live into the founding principles of life, liberty, and the pursuit of happiness and the creational principles of love and the universality of human dignity. I tell you; we are truly not in unfamiliar territory historically as Blacks in America.

Now, the reality is that this pandemic does seemingly have further reach than perhaps any prior sickness within these borders. Yet, the glaring inequalities of suffering, sickness and death connect directly to the historically bifurcated socio-economic structures that make up this young capitalistic culture. Again, we've been here for quite some time.

It is against this backdrop that the critical citizen and committed Christian comes to ask the question, "What does all this mean?" What does it mean when:

1. There are more COVID-19 cases per capita in the US than any other country?
2. The cases are measured not in tens but in tens of thousands.
3. The bulk of the extant cases are found in those ages eighteen to sixty-four.
4. The majority of cases are found within the majority culture, yet the proportion of deaths is greater within the minority cultures.
5. Those with preexisting conditions are most at risk, yet those in the highest office in the land are still adamant about dismantling certain provisions in the affordable care act?
6. Jobs are jeopardized and stimulus checks fall short?
7. Bills are going unpaid and lenders and landlords are rigid with policies?
8. Racism is still prevalent.
9. Sexism is still evident.
10. Ageism is still apparent.

What does all this mean?

I believe the book of Joshua gives us a clue. We engage this narrative at the Jordan. On the heels of all the people crossing over the Jordan successfully, as we glance over the Israelites' shoulders, we see the priests standing firm on the bed of the Jordan River. It is in this moment that God gives Joshua a specific directive. All this is happening while the priests are still standing. I want to encourage some pastors in this season to keep standing. Even when it looks like policy changes are negatively impacting your congregants, keep standing. Even when the money begins to run low, and it looks as though the next few weeks look grim, keep standing. When you get tired, when you get weak, when you just don't feel like it, keep standing. In other words, "after you've done all you can to stand," remember God is with you, and God's "strength is made perfect in weakness."[45]

Even with the powerful imagery of this narrative, there is still one significant question that remains: What does all this mean? This is the refrain throughout

---

45 2 Corinthians 12:9.

Joshua chapter four and I believe the answer is couched within Joshua's declaration and subsequent action. God tells Joshua to have the men from each tribe collect 12 stones from the Jordan to place at Gilgal, where they will lodge for the night. Joshua gives the directive and then declares something significant to them that can be broken down in three parts.

LIFE IS SIGNIFICANT (A SIGN-V. 6A)

First, Joshua lets them know that life is significant. He lets them know that they are laying these stones down that "this may be a sign among you." God wants them to mark this moment in their collective experience. What moments have you marked in your life? We often mark significant moments in life.

1. Christenings and Dedications
2. Baptisms and Bar Mitzvahs
3. Sweet Sixteen and Twenty-First Birthday Parties
4. High School and College Graduations
5. Birthdays and Anniversaries

As a matter of fact, some of these marked moments are so meaningful to us that we get upset, offended, and downright indignant when others do not acknowledge our individual milestones. How much more should we desire for the collective moments to be marked and celebrated? You hear the collective voices rise throughout history from time to time. That collective voice is saying:

1. Remember our fight for independence
2. Remember our battle for states' rights
3. Remember our saga seeking Civil Rights
4. Remember our struggle for gender equality
5. Remember our quest for marriage equality
6. Remember our fight against police brutality

#BlackLivesMatter
#AllLivesMatter
#IMatter
#WEMatter

The collective voices rise throughout history acknowledging the fact that life is significant. Joshua leads these Israelites to collectively leave a marker to memorialize this moment in time.

LEGACY IS SECURE (WHO IS ASKING THE QUESTION-YOUR CHILDREN!-V. 6B)

The second thing we glean from Joshua's declaration is that the Israelites' legacy is secure. Who is asking the question, "what do these stones mean to you?" It is the children—the generations to come. In other words, how you handle your current Jordan reality matters. We have to navigate the Jordan according to God's design. I don't know what your current Jordan is but regardless of what your Jordan is, the aftermath is significant for your legacy. How will the story be told? Who will the key players be? Will your children's children hear of your Jordan experience and appreciate it? Will they witness the markers you have left and understand the significance, or will they merely see it as another missed opportunity or shirked responsibility? How will they see us? We are in this COVID-Jordan moment together. God is marshaling us through together. When we get over, what markers are we going to leave?

LIBERATION IS SUFFICIENT (GOD COMES THROUGH-V. 7A)

In the third instance, Joshua's declaration assures the Israelites that liberation is sufficient. God always comes through. Joshua says very poignantly, tell them the story. Tell them about what God has done for you. You and I might not have a physical Jordan to cross; we might not have been wandering through the physical wilderness for forty years. We may not have had to deal with nations wanting to take us out (then again, maybe we have), but we do know a little something about God's power to come through. Just think back as far as this morning – new mercies were at your doorstep, and they already had the key and alarm code. If you're honest with yourself, God has been better to you than you've been to yourself. God has delivered you from dangers seen and unseen.

1. Sickness
2. Joblessness
3. Homelessness
4. Emotional Pain
5. Psychological Trauma
6. Family Dysfunction
7. Church Hurt
8. Pain and Suffering
9. Misery and Strife

Through it all, God has been the constant.

LEADERSHIP IS SUBSTANTIAL (JOSHUA HAS STONES PLACED IN THE RIVERBED-V. 9)

Before I close this discourse, I must say there is one more thing that arrests my attention in this text. After Joshua's declaration comes a reflective and progressive action. The priests are still in the Jordan River. The stones have been removed from the Jordan by the twelve men, and the priests are still in the Jordan – still standing. In this moment, Joshua shifts from declaration to action and we witness the substance of his leadership. He doesn't, according to the text, receive exact instructions for what he does in verse nine. No, he simply acts on his convictions. I tell you, in this season of scientific data overload, phased approaches to returning to normalcy, and wavering political leaders who are afraid to put people above policy and humanity above economic security, it is good to know God has some committed leaders who are willing to act on their convictions. There is still an assurance from God that true leadership is substantial.

Joshua has twelve stones set up in the Jordan where the priests are standing. Why? Because there is a need for a dual marker—a dual memorial. The committed leader knows the joy of crossing over might be short lived. The marker on the other side of the Jordan is significant, but that can't be our only focus because another Jordan will come. Thanks to Joshua's conviction, those who come to the Jordan will see markers in the river. They may not make it to the other side, but they will know God will be with them while they are in the middle of it. In other words, Joshua understands that you don't get to the mountaintop without going through the valley. Sometimes it's the memory of the valley moments that give you strength when you are on the mountain. To put it another way, you've got to get through death to fully appreciate new life.

Remembering God in Troubled Times: Psalm 20:6–8 (NKJV)

TAMARA KERSEY

May 17, 2020

6 Now I know that the LORD saves His [c]anointed; He will answer him from His holy heaven with the saving strength of His right hand. 7 Some trust in chariots, and some in horses; But we will remember the name of the LORD our God. 8 They have bowed down and fallen; But we have risen and stand upright.

The Psalm read is a psalm of lament of the people shaped into a song to remember and recall the spiritual strength and power of God. In this text, the King is seeking help as he is being menaced and intimidated by those in and outside of his country. In today's times, we could insert ourselves in this text when we see tactics of intimidation within and outside of our own country. Russian hackers are compromising federal and statewide computer data; there is name calling and backlash experienced between political officials and even now there is an invisible enemy that threatens the health of humans around the globe.

In this text, we know they are in a battle because of the reference to chariots and horses and banners with the cries of victory for the battle ahead. In a similar sense, we stand right in the same place as those in the times of this text, we are in our own times alarmed, filled with uncertainty and seemly preparing for battle. In Ancient Israel, the battlefield was a deeply spiritual time of the community coming together for collective prayer, song and unity.

And in vs. 8 we hear a proclamation. A proclamation that reminds us that it is not who has the most destructive weapons, who has the largest and most resources, it is not in sheer human strength and brawn that we experience peace, that we experience freedom and liberty, nor where we even experience triumph, but it is in remember the name that is above every name, the name by which all creation was orchestrated, the name in whom our faith resides. One theologian sums it up this way – Those that make God and God's name their praise, may make God and God's name their trust.

The text tells us that for those in ancient Israel, some trust in chariots, some in horses for their battles and for us today, there are some who trust in financial forecasts, trust the latest news story, trust their almanac and their old wives tales, but for those who have made God the center of our lives, we will remember that we trust only in the name of the Lord.

This text makes it sound simple, but it is not. During times of challenge, struggle, scarcity, and uncertainty, we tend to forget. In those moments when of anxiety, moments of worry, moments of media clips and the latest health reports, for some of us, even momentarily we are susceptible to forget the name of the One who has always provided for us, cared for us, sent blessings unexpectedly, protected us from hurt, harm and danger, opened doors of opportunity and loved us in spite of us. We are susceptible through our human nature that in those moments of life's greatest battles, we forget and fail to remember the name of the Lord.

The mind's capacity to store and recall information at points in time is phenomenal. Psychologists have taught that in order to remember those things we need to know for tests, for life's challenges, we must make mental connections. And, for any of us who spent any time in school, studying for tests for a job or who manage our day to day lives, we all have mechanisms for remembering.

And today, for the days that we live in, we must remember God and who God is. During these days and times, we must be reminded that we cannot use our own strength nor our own wisdom. Today, I'd like to share three ways I believe we can be reminded to Remember God in Troubled Times: Memorize, Visualize and Summarize.

1- Memorize – the Israelites in this text sang songs during their times of trouble. These songs were a collection of their blood sweat and tears, it was a collection of their hope and confidence, their history and experience and from these songs they were able to draw strength from the years of strength and faith of their ancestors. The scriptures and songs of praise were made sacred by those who have come before us. There have been pandemics before our time, there have been wars and tragedy before our time and its through scripture and song that fellow believers were able to sing: "Lift Every Voice and Sing,"[46] "I am on the Battlefield for my Lord"[47] and the memories of those song reminded our people that God is always by our side.

2- Visualize – in v. 6 David says: Now know I that the LORD saveth his anointed; he will hear him from his holy heaven with the saving strength of his right hand. It was also David who wrote in Psalm 37, I was young and now I am old, yet I have never seen the righteous forsaken or their children begging bread. Our faith journeys have brought us to the place of belief that we have now. For some of us, it's been through tests or trials, through tragedy, sickness, for some of us it's been the way that the Lord protected and guided us, kept us, showed us places and things, by our own merit we would have never experienced. When you know without a shadow of a doubt that you've seen the Lord's hand on your life, you've seen doors opened, you've seen God provide for you in miraculous, you can look back on those times and you are able to see that that God has been with you all along and God will not leave nor forsake you.

3- Summarize – 1 Peter 3:14- and 15 But even if you should suffer for righteousness' sake, you are blessed. "And do not be afraid of threats, nor be troubled." 15 But sanctify the Lord God in your hearts, and always be ready to give a defense to everyone who asks you a reason for the hope that is in you,

When we are visited by trouble, troubled relationships, crises and even this pandemic, we should be reminded that trouble is a test. It's a time of searching and sifting that we may draw nearer to God. That we let go of our preconceived notions of what is required and seek what God requires.

Trouble may come and shake us to our core, but will we remember God and who God is in our lives? In those times where you or those you are connected to begin to momentarily forget the power that is in God and God alone you can begin to summarize.

In the culture of the black church, we call it testifying and to have a testimony. And although we may not be in traditional worship service we can still testify. When King David, the writer of this Psalm was greatly distressed and was under constant threats, David encouraged himself in the Lord.

---

46 "Lift Every Voice and Sing." Also known as the Black National Anthem. Written by James Weldon Johnson and set to music by J. Rosamond Johnson.

47 Traditional Gospel Song.

And we too can summarize what God has done for us to encourage ourselves in the Lord. We remember by declaring the good works God has done in our lives. We can declare from the sanctuary from our homes as we remember the God who is the great I am. Some trust in chariots, some trust in horses but we remember, depend and lean on the name of the Lord our God.

Singing Without a Sanctuary: Psalm 27:4–6 (NASB)

AARON MARBLE

April 26, 2020

One thing I have asked from the Lord, that I shall seek: that I may dwell in the house of the Lord all the days of my life, to behold the beauty of the Lord and to meditate in His temple. For in the day of trouble He will conceal me in His tabernacle; in the secret place of His tent; He will hide me; He will lift me up on a rock. And now my head will be lifted up above my enemies around me, and I will offer in His tent sacrifices with shouts of joy; I will sing, yes, I will sing praises to the Lord.

On April 15th, 2019, the sacred and iconic Notre Dame Cathedral in Paris, France suffered immense damage, due to a structure fire. Priceless relics and artwork suffered smoke damage and were destroyed. Three emergency workers were injured. French president, Emmanuel Macron, indicated that the nation's plan was for the cathedral to be restored partially by 2024. However, a complete and full restoration could require more than two decades. On December 25th, 2019, the cathedral did not host Christmas services for the first time since the French Revolution in the 1700s. However, at 8pm on April 15th, 2020, a year after the fire the bells tolled. Due to COVID-19, the restoration plan has stopped, and worship is not being conducted but there was still a sound in the sanctuary.[48]

---

48 Aurelien Breeden, "One Year After Notre-Dame Fire, an Anniversary Passes Quietly," *The New York Times*, April 15, 2020.

I imagine that some persons in Paris likened the ringing of the bells to an angelic choir. While I read what occurred during the first anniversary of that destructive fire, I was struck by the fact that Notre Dame' s sanctuary was still singing without people. The question we must ask ourselves is can we be a people that sing without a sanctuary?

We know the Church is not the building. We know the Church is the collective of courageous persons who declare Jesus is Lord. However, there is strength and empowerment when all God's children get together. For us who are unapologetically Black and unashamedly Christian, the refuge of the gathering cannot be overstated. For our gathering, is one of the last remaining institutions and physical spaces where we can be Black and don't have to apologize for it. Where we can be Black and not be threatened because of it. So, there is rightful lament that we cannot worship together physically on the Lord's day. It has been our time of solace since we worshipped in the brush harbor.

I know you were married in the sanctuary. I know you were baptized there, and you celebrated your loved one's homegoing. Your baby was dedicated there. Your name is on a pew there and your family helped to build it. I know you helped fry chicken for the building fund. Family, all of those things are valuable and important. However, none of them were done so that you would get attached to a building. Their purpose was never to get you attached to God's place but to God's presence.

During this time while a pandemic is preventing us from gathering in the building, it is pushing us to God's presence. Walter Brueggemann suggests that "one yearning of the human person is for Presence, after all that the world offers is tried and found wanting."[49] Somebody knows that you don't have to be here (in the sanctuary), for God to show up in your there. God has shown up whenever, however, and wherever you needed God to be God. That's why the Psalm writer declared "serve the Lord with gladness; come before His presence with singing."[50] We have reasons to sing even without a sanctuary.

The first reason to sing is that the Lord provides favor. David in verse four of our text shares his desire to dwell in the house of the Lord all the days of his life. To be clear, David's desire is not for a house; he has a palace. Nor is David's desire aimed at securing a divine dwelling place for life after death. David is articulating that he wants permanency in the presence of God. David knew the exclusive, positional presence as experienced in the tent of tabernacle or in the temple. David longs for the presence of God to be permanent and free of the limits of location, because he has experienced the beauty of the Lord.

49 Walter Brueggemann, *The Message of the Psalms: A Theological Commentary* (Minneapolis, MN: Fortress Press, 1984), 153.
50 Psalm 100:2, NKJV.

When you get in God's presence you are introduced to God's favor. That's the best explanation for this phrase "beauty of the Lord." Moses uses the same phrase in Psalm 90:17 when he prays that Israel would experience it and establish their work.[51] It is the request that the Lord would apply beauty, strength, blessing and victory to every ugly situation that arises. For the uncertainty of the Coronavirus isn't the only ugly situation that has crept into the landscape of our lives.

The NFL Draft was on the other night, and seeing the lives of so many young Black men change while they sat at home with their families was inspiring. Many had ugly stories filled with pain and adversity. Yet, the beauty of God's favor is being applied to their ugly situation. Adversity is the climax not the conclusion of their life story. God has called your name and drafted you for service. Regardless of what life may have been and or may be, when God called your name the exchange of your ashes for God's crown of beauty occurred.

This is why you can sing without a sanctuary. God's favor has been making ash for beauty exchanges outside of the sanctuary. Favor is not just for church, if you are only favored at church, that isn't God's favor that's popularity. But when God has given you favor, your name will be spoken well of in meetings you didn't know were scheduled. You will be considered for positions and opportunities you didn't even apply for. When you have favor you can get laid off and still never miss a meal. Favor will restore your marriage and family when it is crumbling. You ought to sing because you have favor.

I sing not only because of God's favor, but because God provides safe harbor. David had his share of political enemies and consequences of personal decisions that led to his need of God's protection. David has to hide in caves and in the wilderness to escape the various trouble in his life. He realizes that the best place of safety is in the presence of God. David says for in the time of trouble the Lord will conceal me. God's presence in your life is safe harbor. It is protection not based on your physical location but based on your spiritual relationship. You will see trouble, but trouble won't see you. In times of trouble God will hide you in plain sight.

When the sisters are getting glammed up and hire a makeup artist, the artist uses various items. They have lipstick, mascara, eye liner, and concealer. The role of concealer is not to remove anything but to cover what is already there. Concealer does not remove a blemish or scar but hides it. I'm so glad that the God we serve is a better concealer than MAC or Maybelline. For in the time of trouble God may not take me out of it but hide me in it.

Yes, there should be a blemish. Yes, there should be a bruise. Yes, there should be a wound and a scar. But the Lord concealed me. I sing because the

---

51   C. Hassell Bullock, "Psalms 1–72," in *Teach the Text Commentary Series*, vol. 1, eds. M. L. Strauss & J. H. Walton (Grand Rapids, MI: Baker Books, 2015), 200.

Lord provides favor, safe harbor, and lastly because the Lord is a raiser. David offers that favor prevails and safe harbor is provided because his head will be lifted above his enemies. His response is to sing to the Lord.

One day a family went out on a speed boat during a casual weekend on the lake. And because they frequented this lake often and were familiar with its currents, they did not wear their life jackets. Unfortunately, the boat's engine malfunctioned and the boat capsized. Everybody knew how to swim except the youngest daughter. They kept searching and frantically screaming her name. Eventually, they heard the voice of the little girl because she was singing. The little girl every night before she went to bed would sing a song because she was afraid of the dark. While she was underneath the boat in the water she just began to sing. It was her singing that led to her rescue. When asked how she survived the little girl credited the ability to keep her head lifted above the water.

That is exactly what the Lord does for us. He keeps our head lifted. If you can just keep your head above the water, then everything will be alright. I know problems are surrounding you. I know enemies may be crowding you. I know you have more questions than you may have answers and that anxiety feels like it's drowning you. But if you can just keep your head lifted. "When the enemy comes in like a flood, the Spirit of the LORD will lift up a standard against him."[52]

As long as you have the Lord's presence you may not have a sanctuary, but you can still sing. You may be sinking, but you can still sing. You may be stressed, but you can still sing. You may be scared, but you can still sing. You may be suffocating, but you can still sing. You may be stifled, but you can still sing. You may be scared, but you can still sing. You may be a sinner, but you can still sing.

---

52 Isaiah 59:19, NKJV.

Pandemic Loneliness: Psalms 66:8–20, John 14:15–21 (NRSV)

ANDRE E. JOHNSON

May 17, 2020

PSALMS 66:8-20 (NRSV)

8 Bless our God, O peoples, let the sound of his praise be heard, 9 who has kept us among the living, and has not let our feet slip. 10 For you, O God, have tested us; you have tried us as silver is tried. 11 You brought us into the net; you laid burdens on our backs; 12 you let people ride over our heads; we went through fire and through water; yet you have brought us out to a spacious place. 13 I will come into your house with burnt offerings; I will pay you my vows, 14 those that my lips uttered and my mouth promised when I was in trouble. 15 I will offer to you burnt offerings of fatlings, with the smoke of the sacrifice of rams; I will make an offering of bulls and goats. (Selah) 16 Come and hear, all you who fear God, and I will tell what he has done for me. 17 I cried aloud to him, and he was extolled with my tongue. 18 If I had cherished iniquity in my heart, the Lord would not have listened. 19 But truly God has listened; he has given heed to the words of my prayer. 20 Blessed be God, because he has not rejected my prayer or removed his steadfast love from me.

JOHN: 14-15-21 (NRSV)

15 If you love me, you will keep my commandments. 16 And I will ask the Father, and he will give you another Advocate, to be with you forever. 17 This is the Spirit of truth, whom the world cannot receive, because it neither sees him nor knows him. You know him, because he abides with you, and he will be in you. 18 "I will not leave you orphaned; I am coming to you. 19 In a little while the world will no longer see me, but you will see me; because I live, you also will live. 20 On that day you will know that I am in my Father, and you in me, and I in you. 21 They who have my commandments and keep them are those who love me; and those who love me will be loved by my Father, and I will love them and reveal myself to them."

"Pandemic Loneliness"

As the COVID-19 pandemic continues, many of us are learning lessons along the way. For instance, many of us are learning what it really important in our lives. We are learning more about our family and friends. We are even learning more about ourselves because for many of us, time has slowed down for us to reflect a little more on ourselves. However, one of the lessons I think many of us are learning as we continue to stay at home, shelter in place, and practice social distancing is what it means for us to be alone. During the time of a pandemic, there is a new meaning to being alone and being lonely. So, I came asking on today, anybody alone? Anybody lonely?

I know, if you are like me, sometimes I can have a good time all by myself. Sometimes I can get away from everything and everybody and enjoy the peace and quiet only that being alone can bring. This is usually when I meditate or pray or just read a book or read scripture. It is a time of renewal and refreshment as I relax in the Lord and enjoy God's presence in the stillness and quiet of the day.

So, getting away and being by oneself alone with our thoughts can be a good thing. Sometimes we need to get away from the crowds. We sometimes need to get away from the cell phones, emails, and text messages. We sometimes need to get away from the negative forces trying to conquer our spirits. We sometimes need to get away from the strife and mess that can consume our lives. Yeah, being alone by oneself is sometimes a good thing, but there is being alone and being lonely because there is a big difference in being alone and being lonely.

One can be by oneself and not be lonely. One can be single and not be lonely. One can sleep by oneself every night and yet not be lonely. On the other hand, one can have friends, relatives, and neighbors all around and still be lonely. One can have a good paying and successful job and still be lonely. One can have one's children and grandchildren come and visit all the time and still be lonely. One can be married and sleep next to someone every night and yet still be lonely. Being alone and being lonely are two different things. There are some people who are alone, but many more people are lonely.

We can be lonely in three ways. First, we can be lonely in a physical way. That's more like being alone. We look around and we have no one to be with and we desire the company of someone else. Just another human being to talk to and to share with. No hanky panky, just some good company. Just someone to shoot the breeze with. Just someone to pass time and to be in contact with. Nothing major, just friends or relatives getting together and being together. Just stopping by and watching the ball game or a good movie. Didn't want anything just want to have some company. Being lonely in this phase is quite easy to fix; just go and hang out.

But what are we to do in a pandemic? What are we to do when going out and hanging out is not an option? What are we to do when just being around somebody and just talking with them can help spread the virus?

But there is also emotional loneliness. This is where one desires to be with someone in a more committed and serious relationship. This is where one desires to have a lasting relationship with a person. We mostly think of the single person who is tired of going home alone and sleeping alone. These are the people who want to get married and have the ideal family life. But we must not just limit emotional loneliness to uncoupled people. There are many more emotional lonely people.

These could be married people who desire for their relationship to be the way it used to be. They seem not to be able to get over the hump that has blocked their relationship from being full of the love and bliss it once was. These could be teen-age girls or boys who, in their emotional loneliness think that by having a boyfriend or girlfriend that would rid them of the hurt they feel by being lonely. "If only I could have a person to care for," they say, "I won't be lonely."

This person could be a parent who is estranged from their child and who for the life of them cannot get back to the place where the relationship used to be. There desire is to have that child back into their life and nothing or no one can soothe the empty feeling that she or he feels that's deep down in the pits of their souls. This person could be anybody who is suffering from being emotional detached or having to deal with someone or something being removed from their lives.

And it becomes even more emotional when it's not our fault. Someone dies that we loved and cared for. Someone writes us a dear John or dear Jane letter telling us that it's over. Someone giving us the pink slip saying thanks but today is your last day. Someone who has been a friend for years all of a sudden becomes a foe.

And it is this emotional loneliness that has been expose ever so clearly during the pandemic. Truth of the matter is that many folks have discovered that they were emotionally lonely for a long time. It's then that we discover that the outlets we use to have to get away from the pain, from the emotional toil, from the loneliness just won't work in a pandemic. So, we find ourselves stuck in a house; in a place we would rather not be. Stuck with dealing with stuff we would rather suppress; stuck with our emotions, stuck with our grief, stuck with our pain; and stuck with the truth that we actually have been lonely for a long time, we just before the pandemic, had stuff to cover it all up.

Emotional loneliness can be tough but there is still one more type of loneliness and that's spiritual loneliness. This usually happens when everything else in life seems to be working out fine. One has a great job, money in the bank, relationships with spouse, family, and even co-workers are happy and healthy. Everything is working out at school, grades are good, and friends are all around and even the teachers like you. Everything one touches seems to turn into gold but yet, that person knows something is missing. That person knows that there is a joy that's not being received. The peace that passes all understanding is passing by and only that person truly knows it.

For the person of faith, what is missing is a relationship with the One who calls, commissions, and comforts. In other words, this person may be in fellowship, but out of relationship. This person can't feel anything, hear nothing, or do nothing because nothing is coming through and prayers don't seem to be answered. So, frustration sits in and people don't know what to do with this person because she, he, or they seems to have it all together. These people are spiritually lonely and until they tackle the spiritual questions, "who am I" and "what God means to me" the loneliness will continue.

Maybe Jesus knew that the disciples would start to feel this way after he left them. Jesus was giving his farewell discourse. He knew the time was getting near and he had a date with the cross on Calvary. So, in good teacher tradition, he was giving some last words to the disciples. He told them that he must go because he had in essence a building project to do. He had to prepare some places for them because in his Father's house are many mansions and if it were not so, he would have not told them. In other words, I must leave to prepare a place for you, so that where I am, you can be also. I can't get this building project going if I stay here, I must go and leave you here.

But Jesus knew that this still didn't sit too well with the disciples. He knew that he was leaving, but the disciples didn't want to except this. The disciples liked the way things were going and just didn't fully understand why he had to leave in the first place. Why can't we just keep it going like it is? Why do you have to leave and leave us here? Why can't it be like it is now forever?

And the reality of life is that while some things change, sometimes the change is for the good. Even though the disciples didn't see it, Jesus had to leave them and finish the work that he had to do. And even in our lives, when change comes, we may fight and buckle against the change. We may give every excuse in the book about why "the change" won't work and what "the change" is not going to do. We may try to shoot "the change" down and get mad at the people that see what we don't see. We may talk bad about "the change" without truly understanding that "the change" will be for the better.

We are going to miss how it used to be. We are going to miss our friends. We are going to miss doing it the way that we used to do it. We are going to miss being around the people we have grown so accustomed to. We are afraid of being alone, but more than that, we are afraid of being lonely.

So, it was with the disciples. Jesus knew that they would be hurt and wrestle with feeling alone. They would also have to battle bouts with being lonely and depressed. This wasn't going to be easy for them. So, Jesus gives them a promise. Jesus says that God will leave with them another Advocate. Another one to fight on their behalf. Another one to stand up and speak to them on their behalf. Another one to care for them and watch out for them. Another one to move mountains and obstacles out of their way. Another one who will speak the Truth. Another one that, like Jesus, the world won't understand. Another one that will be with them and walk with them. Another one who they will know because he will abide in them.

In other words, Jesus is saying that I am not leaving you alone. I am not leaving you as orphans to fend for yourselves. I am not leaving you as some wayward children all by yourselves and alone in the blinding whiteness. I am not leaving you without a witness. I am asking God to send the Advocate, the Counselor, and the Helper, to be with you and to guide you. To move in you and to work in you. To sustain and to free you to be all that God has called you to be.

And the good news today is that the same Advocate, the same Spirit of Truth, the same Helper, the same Holy Spirit is here with us today. The Spirit is definitely here, and we don't have to be lonely. And we don't have to be alone.

Therefore, I came to remind somebody here that the Spirit is with us. We are not orphans. We are not lost children. We don't have to be afraid of change. We are children of the Most High God. We are joint heirs with Christ. We are a royal priesthood and a holy nation. We are a peculiar people. The world doesn't seem to understand what we do and why we do it, but the Spirit of Truth does.

But I know that sometimes we may think and feel we are all alone. Sometimes we may believe that there is no one out there for us and everybody would seem to be against us. Everybody will seem to have something to say about what we do and how we do it. Sometimes it will seem as if we are all alone.

And I don't know about you, but there have been some days that I have wondered where am I going and what am I doing? There have been some days that I wondered would I hold up to the pressures of what people may say. Can I still make it? Can I still take it? There have been days that I have wondered what kind of ministry I am called to do and how long am I called to do it. Lord will anything that I am planning work out.

There have been days that I wondered how we are going to live after Rona; or for that matter, will we have to learn how to live with Rona. How are we as a church are going to come out from all of this? Will it still be the same or do we have to prepare ourselves now for the change? There have been days that I wonder will we make it at all?

So, I openly confess there have been days when I wondered about those things, but I don't wonder about them too long, because it's then I hear the Lord saying, you are not alone. Don't worry about your naysayers, don't worry about your intra-conflict and interpersonal demons. I have left the Advocate to fight for you. I have left the Advocate to defend for you. I have left the Advocate the help you and to strengthen you.

And every now and then when we feel all alone and lonely as exiles in a foreign land, we cry out with the Psalmist in Psalm 66, "O God, you have tested us; you have tried us as silver is tried. You have brought us into the net. You have laid burdens on our backs. You have let people ride over our heads. We went through fire and through the water". So, every now and then we may feel a bit lonely.

But I am quickly reminded that the Spirit is working. And when the Spirit is working, God will have you doing things that you thought you would never do. Have you worshipping in places that you never thought you would worship in. When the Spirit is working, God will have you saying things that you thought you would never say. Going places where you thought you never go.

That's what happens when the Spirit is working, we end up going where God is leading, even in the midst of a pandemic. We end up live streaming and conference calling. We end up Zooming but yet still worshipping. In other words, we end up in our blessed places and we come knowing that the Lord has brought us through. Therefore, we can yell out with the Psalmist in that same Psalm, "yet you have brought us out to a spacious place. We will come into your house with offerings, we will pay our vows that our lips utter, and our mouths promised when we were in trouble."

Because when we allow the Spirit to work, loneliness leaves and depression disappears. When we allow the Spirit to work, relationships are renewed, and hearts become healthy. When we allow the Spirit to work, assurance abounds and blessings bloom. When we allow the Spirit to work, faith is formulated, and love is lifted.

And we can sing with the Psalmist "but truly God has listened, he has given heed to my prayer. Blessed be God because he has not rejected my prayer or removed his steadfast love from me." God works through us. God goes before us. God goes with us. We shall never be alone or lonely. I tell you today, this week, allow the Spirit to work and let the Spirit have its way. And if the Spirit is leading us to change by week's end, don't worry, the change will be for the good.

So, let's embrace the change. Let feel the change, allow the change to strengthen and encourage us. So as long as the Spirit is leading; let us walk in our new destinies and be what God has called us to be.

Amen/Ase`

What's Going On?: Psalm 82:1–6 (NIV)

GLENCIE RHEDRICK

August 15, 2020

1 God presides in the great assembly; he renders judgment among the "gods":

2 How long will you defend the unjust and show partiality to the wicked?

3 Defend the weak and the fatherless; uphold the cause of the poor and the oppressed.

4 Rescue the weak and the needy; deliver them from the hand of the wicked.

5 The 'gods' know nothing, they understand nothing. They walk about in darkness; all the foundations of the earth are shaken.

6 I said, 'You are "gods"; you are all sons of the Most High.'

When Marvin Gaye released the song "What's Going On," back in 1971, he had no idea that it would be relevant today. The nation finds itself stricken with a virus now known as COVID19, a 21st-century pandemic, while still living in a post-slavery pandemic called racism and white supremacy. As the country began to shut down to rid itself of this virus, we began to witness how COVID revealed a nation that lacks care for humanity. This morning let us explore how COVID has exposed this nation to itself and the world. This reality has been one of shock, awe, and dismay, as the nation's ugly and tragic past is oozing out.

On the morning of May 28, I woke up and experienced numbness and sadness to learn that over 100,000 persons died as a result of the virus in such a short span of time. Many people shared their fears, doubts, and anxieties, at the same time, asking the question: can anything good come out of this? All over the city, the state, the nation, and even the world, there was a hush in the air. Many of our foreign friends and allies were wondering, just as we are, what just happened? And, you know, the real question is what's going on? And the perplexing thing is, it is continuing to this very day. This presidency has put the entire world on constant alert. Could this have been a nightmare? Is this still a nightmare? Probably none of us would like to admit it, it is not a nightmare, and it is indeed real.

In the meantime, many of us were working for justice and have continued educating voters regarding why it's necessary to vote. Educating voters on candidate issues and providing a means to get to the polls is essential. This we do, for the sake of justice. My heart is heavy! And My spirit is crying out! So, for this morning, the question for us is two-fold: Where are we? and what do you think is going on?

I think there's a bell going off! Somebody, shaking their head is saying, "I don't hear anything." Brothers and sisters, there is a bell ringing. You can call it a trumpet if you like. The late Rev. Dr. Samuel DeWitt Proctor wrote a book for preachers entitled *The Certain Sound of the Trumpet*.[53] Our bell has been rung! Our bell is ringing. As I witnessed the despair and the expressions on the faces, listened to the hurt, felt the anger, heard the cries from friends and even strangers on the street as cities are burdened with the continued deaths caused by the virus, it is clear that the bell is ringing! As we are approaching a 2020 election, many people are still supporting a president who has little to no regard for the people who have died because of this virus that disproportionately kills people of African Descent. I had to wonder to myself, what myths, what half-truths, and what no truths are they listening to?

I needed a word to help me understand where we, as pastors, clergy, and preachers of the gospel really fit in this scenario. There are many texts that could be fitting for this morning. But the Lord led me to Psalm 82: 1–6. Hear now the sacred text from the New International Version:

God presides in the great assembly; he renders judgment among the "gods": How long will you defend the unjust and show partiality to the wicked? Defend the weak and the fatherless; uphold the cause of the poor and the oppressed. Rescue the weak and the needy; deliver them from the hand of the wicked. The 'gods' know nothing, they understand nothing. They walk about in darkness; all the foundations of the earth are shaken. I said, 'You are "gods"; you are all sons of the Most High

The late Reverend Dr. Taylor wrote *The Sound of a Trumpet*, and Ernest Hemingway wrote *For Whom the Bell Tolls*, both these titles resonated with me.

---

53 Samuel D. Proctor, *The Certain Sound of the Trumpet: Crafting A Sermon of Authority* (King of Prussia: Judson Press, 1994).

Because, my beloved, there is a clarion sound of the trumpet, and the Bell is tolling for thee.[54] To be more specific, the bell is tolling for the clergy. The Psalmist helps me this morning to convey God's word for us. Psalm 82 is talking about a rescue mission for the most vulnerable. The Psalmist is making an indictment regarding our duties as ambassadors for the Most High.

Let me set the stage for us: Imagine, if you will, we are in a courtroom. I guess one might be asking, who is this we; this we are you and me. We are being called into court, not just any court, but the Highest one, the Heavenly court. In this courtroom, we are facing the JUDGE—God. God's appointed prosecutor is representing the plaintiff—the church and the community. As we read the text, it opens with God coming into the courtroom to hear the case set before Him! What's the case, you might ask, it is right there in verse two, "How long will you defend the unjust and show partiality to the wicked?" Let me state it another way from the Message Bible, "You've corrupted justice long enough, you've let the wicked get away with murder."[55] In other words, for us today, we have allowed our people to be swallowed up by thieves and sheep in wolves' clothing. They are in the world without any advocates.

The prosecutor's opening statement is straight from the Psalmist as he quotes it verbatim to present the case to the jurors:

> How Long, how long will you defend the unjust and show partiality to the wicked? How long! We are to Defend the weak and the fatherless; We are to uphold the cause of the poor and the oppressed. We are to Rescue the weak and the needy, And we are to deliver them from the hand of the wicked.[56]

Now, one might ask, what does this have to do with us as clergy, pastors, preachers, and ministers of the gospel and, for that matter, any faith leader? I am so glad you asked! The bell, the trumpet, the alarm has gone off and has been going off. Some of us just got caught in the rhetoric, a misguided noise that has now pushed us back into the 18th century. Some of us became complacent and complicit. I like to use Dr. Barber's words, "some are committing theological malpractice in that what is being said borderlines on saying so much about what God doesn't say and saying so little about what God does say."[57]

I don't know how many of you had the opportunity to see the 21st-century version of the *Birth of a Nation*. Nate Parker provides a clear depiction that the context of the Bible and the relationship of God were used to endorse the institution of slavery. This inhumane and vile treatment of a people, who look like you

---

54 Ernest Heminway. *For Whom The Bell Tolls* Charles Scribner's Sons, 1940.
55 Psalm 82:2 (Message).
56 Ibid. 82:4.
57 William Barber. " *We Can Not Accept This Anymore: The Price of Inequality.*" 2020.

and me was solely for the purpose of economic gain, power, and greed. Not once was Nat Turner ever introduced to the scriptures that spoke of the Prophets Amos and Micah and has much changed today? COVID, as we see it today, is a corrosive and a vivid indictment of defying the laws of God to love all the Creation, including the very ground on which we stand.

Unfortunately, we have a president in the White House who has denounced Dr. Fauci, an expert immunologist whose recommendation was to shut down the country to protect the people in the United States. However, there is a group of Christians that represents a different narrative that in all scenarios supports and endorses the "Let's Make America Great Again," which subscribes to the notion that the virus is fake. They say, "Don't listen to the experts; let's open the country to restore the economy because the COVID-19 is a Hoax."

This group endorsed a return to white dominance; they endorsed an economic society of wealth and power for the 1% to remain at the top. This very pious and religious group of mostly white men and some white women condoned the inappropriateness of this president as they sanctioned inappropriate touching of women and lewd comments about women. And now they are endorsing opening the country with a citizen's right to assemble unprotected in large crowds, in buildings, and, oh yes, in churches. The institution, the church, if you will, is where we come to be healed and to be saved. Now many of the hashtags are coming out of the woodwork to declare that silence will no longer be our mantra. Mr. 45, the bell is ringing. In the Evangelical community that supports his lifestyle and behavior, your bell is being rung. Not as the clarion call for justice, but your bell is being rung to bring an end to the misinterpretation of God's word. The 20th and 21st-century Evangelical community has done to the Bible and to Christianity what the Christian enslavers did to Nat Turner; they are not reading the entire Bible. The Bell is ringing! The trumpet is blowing! The alarm is sounding! What is the duty of watchmen and watchwomen for God's creation?

As the community looks on, the defense attorney approaches the jury box to begin defending the clergy and the faith. The attorney steps up to make the argument. His opening statement: "I am sure your congregants, friends, and relatives are asking, 'Are we in a state of flux?' Some are even fearful! But in spite of the fear, we are a people of hope." For, in verse 6, The psalmist reminds us that we are God, i.e., preachers for our context and that we are children of the Most High. We are to be in partnership with God! So, we have an ordained responsibility to stand for justice, fairness, and equality. So, the answer to the question of what's going on is this: We must continue to advocate, to ensure that health care is available for all citizens and not just a few. What's going on? In this season of COVID, we must be advocates for the community to recognize the health disparities for all Black and Brown and poor people in this country. We must say "no" to the fake news and be vigilant wearing a mask, washing our hands often, physically distancing, and staying away from large crowds. What's going on? We must advocate to ensure that mass incarceration and mass criminalization do not continue to exist; we must work to release the overcrowding of the pods to sustain lives. We must advocate for the release of men and women who are infected by the virus.

What's going on? We must vow to ensure safety for our essential workers as they risk their lives to ensure the safety of many in our hospitals, hotels, restaurants, and waste management systems. What's going on? We must make sure this method of producing free or reduced workforce labor is stopped in its tracks. We must revisit the policies that allow drug screening for jobs, for financial assistance, and now, for some rental and housing programs. These are mechanisms to create a free labor workforce, increase involuntary homelessness, and to eliminate opportunities for educational programs and jobs. We have an obligation to fight for higher wages. What's going on? In a country where we have the freedom to worship, we have a responsibility to stand by a people whose faith is not our own, because they, too, have a right to practice their beliefs just as Christians do! What's going on? We must stand against the mentality that says build a wall and "not in my backyard." We are all strangers and immigrants on this soil that God provides. What's going on? We must stand against corruption, complacency, and contempt. What's going on? We must be obvious and blunt about our belief in the HOLY that calls us to love all that has been created.

What's going on? We are Co-Creators! We are extensions of Jesus; thus, we must preach the message.
Amen and Ase`

I Can't Breathe: Isaiah 40:27–29 (NASB)

R. JANAE PITTS-MURDOCK

June 14, 2020

27 Why do you say, O Jacob, and assert, O Israel, "[Our] way is hidden from the Lord, And the justice due [us] escapes the notice of [our] God"? 28 Do you not know? Have you not heard? The Everlasting God, the Lord, the Creator of the ends of the earth Does not become weary or tired. His understanding is inscrutable. 29 He gives strength to the weary, And to *him who* lacks might He increases power.

In this prophetic utterance to the people of Judah, the prophet Isaiah addresses a beleaguered community, a community still grappling with the residue of exile. While they are presumably on the other side of Babylonian captivity, they are not far beyond the experience of captivity. While there is a sense of freedom from Babylon and freedom from captivity, it seems the community is still working to understand why and how it all happened in the first place. And even though Babylonian captivity is in their rearview mirror, the residual impact of that prolonged experience of displacement and disorientation lingers in the collective memory. the wounds and grief of the experience linger, such that the prophetic response begins in Chapter 40 with God commanding "Comfort, Comfort my people!"

The Elohim, Creator God, the one whose ways are unsearchable, the one whose might is immeasurable says "Comfort, Comfort my people!" This God who is both omnipotent and omniscient, all powerful and all knowing, this God who is right in all things, this God who is holy and perfect...this God commands the divine messengers to Comfort God's people. This command to Comfort God's people contradicts the image of the rule of order God. The God of domination and submission. This God says COMFORT my people. Stop with your typical prophetic visions and interpretations, stop with your invectives and your reprimands. Stop with the critique. Stop telling the people what they're doing too much of, and what they're not doing enough of. Stop telling them what they did wrong and what they didn't do well enough. Stop reminding them of their areas of improvement and their pockets of imperfection. Just stop. God tells the divine messengers, "Right now, in this moment, I want you to Comfort my people. Speak tenderly to my people. Comfort my people." It's as if God says, listen for their cries. Listen for their groanings. And offer them comfort. Not flowery words, not empty symbols, not social media posts. Comfort my people. Be present. Be attentive. Be open. Be affirming. Be encouraging. Be thoughtful. Be kind. Comfort my people.

I must admit, in all of my years of Sunday morning church going, midweek bible Study attendance, Sunday school participation, local, state and national convention delegating, and vacation bible school going, I've found that comfort language is mostly relegated to funerals. I've heard sermons on repentance, praise, triumph, liberation, lament, heaven, hell, women, men, children, relationships, money but not a whole lot of comfort. Even while listening to God for today's message, I wrestled with this notion of Comfort. I wanted to preach protest. I wanted to preach uprising. I wanted to preach resistance. And the Holy Spirit challenged me by saying, "To recognize battle-fatigue in our communities and fail to provide triage or care is to participate in the problem and not the solution. That kind of neglect perpetuates woundedness and not healing." Comfort my people.

It is the aim of racism and white supremacy to choke the literal and figurative life out of African Americans and Hispanic/Latino people. We are suffocating on the front lines of health disparity, wealth disparity, education disparity, and any other metric for human flourishing in this country. This is not because we are inherently deficient. We are not. It is not because we lack initiative. We do not. It is not because we lack competence. We do not. When afforded fewer resources and fewer opportunities, we remain competitive and even outperform our white siblings in some areas. But climbing a mountain in the middle of the desert with nothing but a pair of Jordans and one hand tied behind our backs is exhausting, especially when our white siblings get two hands, pulleys, parachutes, and Perrier.

And why is it this way? It is this way because racism and white supremacy are the demonic presence that bathe every institution in this Country…and too many of our churches too. And those demons of racism and white supremacy infect every non-resisting person and institution with varying degrees of hatred, denial, indifference, and ignorance. They inflict the perpetual brutality of inequity and systemic oppression, and they have molested even our religious institutions into surrendering to their cause. We have reduced the systems of racism and white supremacy to individual acts of consciousness. Yet racism is woven into the fabric of this nation and white supremacy is the codification and systematizing of that racism in the foundations of every institution...even down to the manufactured derogatory narratives that some of us Black folk repeat and perpetuate. And just like George Floyd on a Minneapolis sidewalk and Eric Garner on a Staten Island sidewalk, we show up with the weight of these demons on our backs saying, "I can't breathe!" I can't breathe.

Once again, this phrase haunts the airways. "I can't breathe." It's on billboards and cardboard signs. It is spray painted on the sides of buildings. It's on t-shirts. Backpacks. And as I watch well-meaning people sling it like a new catch phrase or political slogan, and the capitalist machine profit from it, I sometimes feel like, '"[Our] way is hidden from the LORD, And the justice due [us] escapes the notice of our God"' (v.27). I can't breathe. I know that I'm not alone this morning. I know that there are numbers of you watching and listening who are exhausted by the same racist record on repeat. There are scores of you who feel like voting rights icon Fannie Lou Hamer, who said, "I'm sick and tired of being sick and tired."[58] There are numbers of you who are ready for a change to come. Maybe you too have felt like '"[Our] way is hidden from the LORD, And the justice due [us] escapes the notice of our God."' (v.27).

Justice is due us! Justice is due us for centuries of uncompensated and under-compensated labor. Justice is due us for generations of violence and terrorism by colonizers and their descendants. Justice is due us for the denial of our education, the breeding of our women, and the assault on our men. Justice is due us for the defiling of our children. Justice is due us for the spit in our faces, the bombs in our churches, the suppression of our vote, and the redlining of our neighborhoods. Justice is due us for the over-policing of our neighborhoods, the exaggerated 9-1-1 calls, and the militarization of law enforcement. Justice is due us for the open display and celebration of symbols of white domination and domestic terrorism. Justice is due us for the delay of equitable access to every single wealth building resource in this country. Justice is due us for the imprisonment of a liberating gospel by white evangelicalism. Justice is due us for the pacifying words of racial reconciliation absent the regard for repentance and reparation.

Justice is due us! Sometimes I feel like "Our way is hidden from the LORD, And the justice due us escapes the notice of our God."

---

58 Fannie Lou Hamer, "I'm Sick and Tired of Being Sick and Tired," in *The Speeches of Fannie Lou Hammer: To Tell It Like It Is*, eds. Maegan Parker and Davis W. Houck (Jackson: University Press of Mississippi, 2011), 57–64.

This is the Biblical terrain where the Spirit brought me for relief as recent events have returned us to the all too familiar phrase, "I Can't Breathe." Isaiah 40:27–29:

> [27] Why do you say, O Jacob, and assert, O Israel, "My way is hidden from the LORD, And the justice due me escapes the notice of my God"? [28] Do you not know? Have you not heard? The Everlasting God, the LORD, the Creator of the ends of the earth Does not become weary or tired. His understanding is inscrutable. [29] He gives strength to the weary, And to *him who* lacks might He increases power.

Isn't it just like God to meet us in the middle of pandemic, meet us in the middle of battle-fatigue, meet us in the middle of protest for a moment of refreshment. The Lord comforts us with 4 things today:

1. God's got time! – The Everlasting God, the LORD, the Creator of the ends of the earth does not become weary or tired. In other words, God always has time for us. Our cares. Our concerns. Our worries. God never gets weary or tired of us. People get tired. And people get tired of us. People grow weary of our groanings and irritated with our complaints. People get busy attending to their personal lives and run out of time for us. But not God. God is never too busy to hear, listen, and get involved in our lives. God's got time.

2. God's understanding is beyond our understanding. – Comfort my people and let them know that my understanding is beyond their understanding. God knows the answer to every question and has the solution to every problem. There is depth of knowledge, depth of wisdom and depth of knowing in God. We may not understand fully what is happening and why things are the way they are. Don't overwhelm yourself with not knowing because God knows. God sees ahead of us. God understands beyond us. God comprehends past, present, and future at the same time while caring for the details of each specific individual. God's understanding is beyond our understanding.

3. God gives strength to the weary. – Comfort my people that I give strength to the weary. I give strength to those who are tired. I give strength to fight, strength to march, strength to protest, strength to boycott. To resist. To organize. To speak up. I give strength to the weary, those who have become worn down by oppression, the pressure of systematic injustice, weary overwhelmed and worn out. I find them, pick them up and refresh them with my word and my presence. I give strength to the weary. If you have become weary do not consider it a liability or a disadvantage. Rather, consider it as an avenue to draw closer to God. Consider

it an invitation to greater care from God. This God gives strength to the weary.

4. God increases power to the one who lacks might. – Power is a tricky word in our contemporary context. Power reflects the maligned, impure, and reckless decimation of people groups. Power in this nation has been used recklessly to dominate and control, to harm whole groups of people. But that is not the kind of power that God gives. This is not the power that comes from the White House. It does not come from CEOs. This power does not come with a badge or a gun. But this is the kind of power that God shares with God's creation. God's power is transformative, renewing, and revitalizing. Tears of joy came to my eyes as I considered just how much power Black people in America have. No, we don't have WHITE power, but we have transformative power. Like you, I have to work daily to free myself from an intoxication with definitions of strength and success created by systems constructed to protect white superiority, preoccupations with that which is marked with superficial signs of success and value wars against the truth of a liberating gospel. Do you know what kind of power Black folks have? No, it's not white power, it's transformative power. Do you know what kind of power it takes to survive 400 years of intentional exclusion? Do you know what kind of power it takes to be mistreated and abused and refuse surrender? We have this kind of power because God gifts it to us. God increases power to the one who lacks might.

God comforts us with these reminders that God's got time for us, God's understanding is beyond our understanding, God gives strength to the weary and God increases power to those who have no might.

Dr. Maya Angelou, in her poem "Still I Rise," captures the essence of who we are as a people comforted by God.

> Just like moons and like suns,
> With the certainty of tides,
> Just like hopes springing high,
> Still I'll rise.

We will rise from this moment. We will rise from our condition. We will rise from these catastrophes. How do I know? [28] Do you not know? Have you not heard? The Everlasting God, the LORD, the Creator of the ends of the earth Does not become weary or tired. His understanding is inscrutable. [29] He gives strength to the weary, And to *him who* lacks might He increases power.

Building Houses in Babylon: Jeremiah 29: 4–11 (NKJV)

C. DEXTER WISE III

April 19, 2020

[4] Thus says the Lord of hosts, the God of Israel, to all who were carried away captive, whom I have caused to be carried away from Jerusalem to Babylon:

[5] Build houses and dwell in them; plant gardens and eat their fruit.

[6] Take wives and beget sons and daughters; and take wives for your sons and give your daughters to husbands, so that they may bear sons and daughters—that you may be increased there, and not diminished.

[7] And seek the peace of the city where I have caused you to be carried away captive, and pray to the Lord for it; for in its peace you will have peace.

[8] For thus says the Lord of hosts, the God of Israel: Do not let your prophets and your diviners who are in your midst deceive you, nor listen to your dreams which you cause to be dreamed.

[9] For they prophesy falsely to you in My name; I have not sent them, says the Lord.

[10] For thus says the Lord: After seventy years are completed at Babylon, I will visit you and perform My good word toward you, and cause you to return to this place.

[11] For I know the thoughts that I think toward you, says the Lord, thoughts of peace and not of evil, to give you a future and a hope.

In this sermon, Rev. Wise positions the pandemic as a time of upheaval and change. Drawing from the exilic conditions suffered by Judah, Rev. Wise warns us that in seasons of upheaval and change, who we listen to is important. Grounded in the godly counsel of Jeremiah, he suggests we can do four things while waiting on our change to come.

When a major change occurs in your life, when do you know that it is time to make a major adjustment to your life? If it is a minimal change, you may have to make no change at all. If it is a minor change, you may only have to make a minor change. However, if it is a major change, you may understand that you will have to make a major adjustment. But the question is: "How do you know when to make that change?"

For example, when you travel to a foreign country, how long do you have to be there before you should learn the language? When you cross over into a different time zone, how long should you be there before you change your watch to the local time? When you move to another house, how long should you be out of your old house before you start forwarding your mail to your new house? When you get married, how long should it be before you change your name? When you transfer to another city, how long should it be before you change the area code on your phone? When you check into a hotel, how long should you plan to stay before you put your clothes in the hotel drawers? Something has changed in your life, but how do you know when to change your life?

This was the dilemma of the people of Judah in the days of the prophet Jeremiah. King Nebuchadnezzar of Babylon had ransacked Jerusalem. He had taken the royal family and the middle and upper-class people captive. He had stolen the vessels from the temple and carried them back to Babylon. The people left in Jerusalem were wondering when the captives were coming back. Those who were held captive were wondering when they were going to get a chance to go back.

None of the Hebrews who were taken to Babylon wanted to be there because Babylon was an unfamiliar place they had never been before. Babylon was an ungodly place that did not honor their God. Babylon was an uncertain place that posed too many unanswerable questions. Babylon was an undesirable place they just did not want to be. Yet, there they were captives in Babylon and had no idea how long they would be there.

Of course, their situation was far more severe than ours. We are on lock down and can't leave home. The people of Judah were in exile and couldn't go home. We are stuck in the comforts of our own home. They were in a foreign land without a home. We can order carry out from our couch. They had their couches carried out. We can Facetime our loved ones who live far away. They would never see or hear from their loved ones ever again. Of course, their situation was far more severe than ours, but at the same time, it is amazingly similar. Like them, we, too have had a major invasion hit our nation. Like them, we too have suddenly found ourselves in an unfamiliar place, an ungodly place, an uncertain place, and an undesirable place.

Like them, we have had two types of prophets advising us what to do. They had a prophet named Hananiah, who pronounced a rosy prophesy that the exile would only last for two years. He prophesied that everyone would be able to return, the kingdom would be re-established, and the people would be restored. Then, opposed to him was the prophet Jeremiah. He declared a realistic prophecy. He predicted that the exiles would return, but instead of two years, it would take seventy years.

So, there you have it. A choice between rosy and reality. There are the rosy prophets of profits. They predict that the virus will just go away in the springtime. That fifteen cases will go down to zero. That we have this virus completely under control. That we can go back to normal in less than a month. Then, on the other hand, there are the realistic prophets of facts. They say that instead of a month, this may last for a year. For them, it is not admitting defeat. It is reality. It is not a matter of doubt. It is reality. It is not a lack of faith. It is reality. It is not a spirit of fear. It is reality. It's temporary, but it's a long temporary.

Needless to say, the people chose to listen to Hananiah's rosy prophesy and sought to kill Jeremiah. But the fact is that Hananiah was wrong and died within a year. Jeremiah was right and the people of Judah spent seventy long years as exiles in Babylon. Since Jeremiah was right, maybe we should listen up and listen in on what he advised the people of Judah to do once it was clear that they would be forced to live in this new Babylonian reality for a while. So, if this is our reality, Jeremiah, what would you recommend that we do?

The first thing he said to do was build houses. That is, customize, don't compromise.

You don't have to settle for Babylon, but you may have to settle down in Babylon for a minute. Don't buy or rent a house because those houses were made by the Babylonians for Babylonians in a different time. But you build a house from scratch customized to make it possible for you to live there. It might remind you of your house back home, but this has got to be a different house because you are in a different place. Create your own space in their place. This is what Daniel did when he refused to eat the king's meat.[59] This is what the Hebrew boys did when they refused to bow.[60]

We may have to worship online, but we are still going to worship. We may have to practice social distancing, but we are still going to stay connected. We may not have money, but we are still going to give. We may have to stay at home, but we can still work from home. Just because you are in a new and different place, doesn't mean that you have to compromise your values, integrity, identity, destiny, or vision. Build houses – Customize, don't compromise.

59 Daniel 1:8–16.
60 Daniel 3:13–18.

Secondly, Jeremiah recommended that the exiles plant gardens. That is, grow, don't gripe. You have a choice. You can gripe about it, or you can grow because of it. Planting was the last thing on the Hebrews' mind because planting takes time. Still, Jeremiah said: "Don't go to the farmers' market and buy it. Plant your own garden and grow it." Planting means staying in one place. That's why you have to commit to remain there long enough to harvest what you have sown. Planting means that where you are is fertile. Moses never commanded the Israelites to plant gardens in the wilderness. They had to wait until they got to the Promised Land for that.

But Jeremiah says: "Even though where you are is a place of captivity, it is still fertile ground." As bad as Babylon may seem to be, it is fertile enough to grow some major fruit. And while you are there, plan to grow patience. Plan to grow creativity. Plan to grow self-reliance. Plan to grow compassion. Plan to grow a stronger prayer-life. Plan to grow in the knowledge of the word and faith.

Thirdly, Jeremiah advised the exiles to take wives. Translation – Multiply, don't die. Don't let exile be the reason that you cease to exist. We have to be like comedian Robin Harris' Bebe Kids: "We don't die, we multiply."[61]

We must continue to exist for the sake of continuity. If all of the people who were taken captive did not have families and children while in Babylon, they would have all died out within seventy years. What you have and who you are is worth saving and continuing. We must continue to exist in order to produce durability. Any person who survives this ordeal will be a stronger person. Those who come out on the other side will be able to fight off what previous generations could not. We must continue to exist to give us a testimony. Those who survive this ordeal will have a testimony second to none.

Fourthly, the prophet urged the exiles to increase while there. Put another way, they were to expect productivity and prosperity in captivity; that you may be increased there, and not diminished. You are in Babylon, but you still have skills. You are creative craftsmen. You are enterprising entrepreneurs. You are bold builders. You are able administrators. You are talented teachers. You are community developers. You are skilled scientists. You are praying priests.

Remember how the Hebrew men[62] were written up by their Babylonian supervisors with the hope that they would be thrown in the fire? Not only did they survive the fire and come out without even the smell of smoke on them, but the King also gave them a raise! As strange as it may sound, Babylon does not have to mean your ruin. It can mean you are about to get a raise. I don't know about you, but I'm claiming my raise!

---

61 Robin Harris. https://www.youtube.com/watch?v=nE-AHDt-foQ
62 Shadrach, Meshach, and Abednego in Daniel 3.

Fifthly and finally, the prophet relayed these words of God to them: "I know the plans I have for you..." (KJV) So you should trust the Architect even though you have never seen the plans.

> 11 For I know the thoughts that I think toward you, says the Lord, thoughts of peace and not of evil, to give you a
>
> future and a hope.

You may not know, but I know.

> "Eye has not seen, nor ear heard,
> Nor have entered into the heart of man
>
> The things which God has prepared for those who love
>
> Him." (I Corinthians 2: 9)

Who would ever think that a baby named Moses thrown in the river would save a nation? But that was all in His plan. Who would ever think that a little shepherd boy named David would be the king of Israel? But that was all in His plan. Who would ever think that an unsuspecting, unassuming virgin girl named Mary would be the mother of the Son of God? But that was all in His plan. Who would ever think that a child named Jesus laying in a manger in Bethlehem would be the Savior of the world? But that was all in His plan. Who would ever predict that a persecutor named Saul would become a preacher named Paul? But that was all in His plan. Who would ever guess that a beautiful young Hebrew woman named Esther would become the Queen of an empire? But that was all in His plan.

Who would ever imagine that a seamstress named Rosa Parks, sitting on a bus in Alabama, would start a movement when she refused to move? But that was all in His plan. Who would ever foresee that a boy named Barack Obama born in Hawaii to a white woman and an African man, would grow up to be the first Black president of the United States? But that was all in His plan. It was all in His plan.

God, I don't see where You are going. I don't see what You are doing. I don't understand what is happening. But since You had sense enough to plan how to set the sun on fire and it's still burning. Hang the moon in the night sky and it's still glowing. Place the earth on its axis and it's still turning. Position the stars in the sky and they are still twinkling. Plant grass on the ground and it's still growing. Launch birds in the air and they are still flying. Put ants in the dirt and they are still crawling.

You surely have great plans for me. So, I trust You to work it out. I trust You to see me through. I trust You to provide a way. I trust You to open a door. I trust

You to take care of my family. I trust You to heal my body. I trust You to build a fence around me. I trust You to meet my need.

> Tis so sweet to trust in Jesus.
> Just to take Him at His word.
> Just to rest upon His promise.
> Just to know thus saith the Lord.
> Jesus, Jesus how I trust Him.
> How I proved Him o'r and o'r.
> Jesus, Jesus precious Jesus
> Oh, for grace to trust Him more.

How Long? We Can't Breathe: Habakkuk 1:2 (NIV)

CORY JONES

May 31, 2020

2 How long, LORD, must I call for help, but you do not listen? Or cry out to you, "Violence!" but you do not save?

There's an old saying that goes like this: "When white America catches a cold, black America gets pneumonia." The last few months have been devastating. The economy tanked significantly, millions have lost jobs, we've been forced to keep distance, lives have been lost, and families have been turned upside down. But, "when white America catches a cold, black America gets pneumonia." We've had to deal with higher death rates and the burden of this entire pandemic has affected our communities in a deeper way. We caught pneumonia. We've been told to work from home. It's hard to work from home if you're a hairstylist. It's hard to work from home if you're a server at a restaurant. It's hard to work from home if you work at the mall that's now closed or the local store and your hours have been cut. We caught pneumonia.

The truth is that we're not just dealing with pneumonia. We're dealing with double pneumonia. From a medical perspective, pneumonia affects one lung. Double pneumonia affects both lungs. It's serious and can be fatal. One lung caught the dire effects of COVID-19. We've been hit the hardest. And while we were confronting the challenges of coronavirus in one lung, we caught pneumonia in the other lung. In February, a 25-year-old African American young man named Ahmaud Arbery was jogging in Brunswick, GA. He was viewed as a threat and ended up losing his life at the hands of three white men.[63] In March, Breonna Taylor was shot during a "no-knock" raid of her home. In fact, police had the person they were looking for in custody before the raid even happened.[64] So, we have a jogger and a young lady at home asleep both dead.

The other day Christian Cooper, an African American man, was bird watching in Central Park. Amy Cooper was there as well. Her dog was off the leash in an area where all dogs were supposed to be on a leash. When Christian Cooper requested that the dog be placed on a leash an altercation developed. Amy Cooper threatened to call the police and tell them that an African American male threatened her life. It was all caught on camera. There was no thought in her mind that an incident like that could have killed Christian Cooper. There was no thought in her mind that an incident like this could have gotten Christian Cooper arrested or harassed. Her privilege would not allow her to see how her actions could potentially take the life of another human being.[65]

And now, we are forced to confront another incident. George Floyd was arrested in Minneapolis. While in handcuffs, three officers hold him down with one specific officer placing his knee on Floyd's neck. He screamed in pain. He cried that he couldn't breathe. He even called out to his mother. His nose began to bleed. His body became numb. He died from the incident.[66] The scene was reminiscent of Staten Island when police choked Eric Garner.[67] His cries of "I can't breathe" were ignored as he succumbed to the chokehold. Isn't it interesting that one symptom of double pneumonia is difficulty breathing? "I can't breathe" describes the societal double pneumonia we are experiencing right now. We've got coronavirus in one lung and racism in the other lung. And we hear the cries throughout the country, "I can't breathe!"

---

63 Angela Barajas and Martin Savidge. "Ahmaud Arbery Killing being Investigated as Federal hate Crime, Family Attorney Says," *CNN*. May 26, 2020. https://www.cnn.com/2020/05/25/us/ahmaud-arbery-doj-hate-crime-investigation/index.html

64 Christina Carrega. FBI Opens an Investigation into the Death of Breonna Taylor. May 22, 2020. https://abcnews.go.com/US/fbi-opens-investigation-death-breonna-taylor/story?id=70829091

65 Samuel Getachew. You Shouldn't Need a Harvard Degree to survive Birdwatching While Black. May 28, 2020. https://www.washingtonpost.com/outlook/2020/05/28/christian-cooper-harvard-birdwatching/

66 Dalton Bennett, Joyce Sohyun Lee , and Sarah Cahlan. "The Death of George Floyd: What Video and Other Records Show About His Final Minutes," *Washington Post*. May 30, 2020. https://www.washingtonpost.com/nation/2020/05/30/video-timeline-george-floyd-death/

67 Eric Garner died at the hand of police on July 17, 2014, at the hands of Daniel Pantaleo. Pantaleo choked Garner to death.

One of my white classmates reached out to express her empathy and outrage at the situation. I responded to her by simply saying, "We're tired." The same thing has gone on for too long. In 1955, a fourteen-year-old boy named Emmett Till was killed for what he allegedly did to a white woman named Carolyn Bryant. He was heard saying, "Bye baby" as he and his friends left the store. However, she claimed that he grabbed her, made lewd advances, and wolf-whistled at her. It was not until Carolyn Bryant was at the end of her life that she admitted that Emmitt Till did none of those things to her. That young boy died because of false testimony. And in 2020, we have another white woman threatening to call the police and tell them that a black man did something he did not do. We're tired.

CNN was on the ground covering the reaction to George Floyd's murder. There were two reporters in the area, a white man named Josh Campbell and another Omar Jimenez (Black and Latino). Josh Campbell's crew was treated with respect and were permitted to report from an agreed upon location. Jimenez' crew had a different experience. Although they identified themselves as the press, they were arrested.[68] The situation was so blatant that the Minnesota Governor had to apologize for their actions. One journalist was treated one way and the other journalist was treated another way. One group can eat in the restaurant and the other has to go to the back. One group drinks from this water fountain and the other drinks from that one. One group rides on the front of the bus and the other rides in the back. We're tired.

I'm reminded of the prophet Habakkuk. Habakkuk is mixed with laments and responses. The prophet laments to God and God responds back to the prophet. This is an interesting book because with most prophets God gives the prophet the word to give back to the people. In addition, it is God who is typically complaining about the behavior of the people. However, in this book, it is a debate going on between the prophet and God. The prophet is giving his side of the argument and God is responding back with God's side of the argument.

I love Habakkuk because, in Hebrews 4:16, we are told to come boldly before the throne of grace so that we may get mercy and find grace to help in the time of need. Habakkuk is the embodiment of this scripture. Habakkuk has some issues with God. Habakkuk has a problem with God. So, Habakkuk brings his issues to God. His question is simple. "How long Lord?" How long do I have to cry before you will listen? How long Lord? When are you going to hear me? How long Lord? I'm crying out to you. There's violence out here and yet you will not save. How long Lord? Why do you idly sit back and look at all the wrong that's going on? How long Lord? I've got all this stuff going on around me. Destruction. Violence. Strife. Contention. It's all around me. How long Lord?

---

68 Police Arrest CNN Correspondent Omar Jimenez and Crew on Live Television. *CNN You-Tube*, May 29, 2020. https://www.youtube.com/watch?v=ftLzQefpBvM

And watch this piece. The real issue for Habakkuk is injustice. Justice promotes equity and harmony in a community. "Justice is the standard by which the benefits and penalties of living in a society are distributed." Justice "aims at creating a community where all classes of people maintain their human rights." That's justice. Habakkuk is shouting out to God, "There ain't no justice going on!" Look at verse 4. The law is powerless (paralyzed) and justice never goes forth. The wicked surround the righteous and because of that, justice ends up being perverted. God, I have some issues.

I love Habakkuk! Habakkuk is that dude! Habakkuk is speaking thousands of years ago about what's happening in 2020. O Lord, how long? How long is it going to be like this? How long do we have to continue this cycle? How long will injustice prevail? How long will evil be around us? How long do we have to deal with all of this? God, we can't breathe! What do you do when you can't breathe?

In the middle of all of this, there is some good news if you're willing to look for it. One of the reasons Habakkuk is complaining to God is because he recognizes God has the power to do something about the situation. Now some may not find good news in that because that is exactly the reason Habakkuk is complaining. God has the power and is choosing not to do anything about the situation. However, if you view this scripture through another set of lenses, you may see something else. If I view scripture through the eyes of a God that cares about me and loves me, then I know God has something up God's sleeve. I may not understand how, and I may not understand the divine strategy, but my faith tells me that God has to be up to something!

So, even when I don't see the change I'm looking for yet, I can still celebrate knowing that God has the power and God is able! Can I talk real with you? Knowing that God is able has gotten me through some things before. There was stuff I couldn't have gotten through if I didn't know/believe God was able. There was mess I was involved in and would not have been able to be pulled out of if I didn't know God was able. I'm talking to somebody. You wouldn't have been able to survive if you didn't know God was able. You would not have made it if you didn't know God was able. It's ok to be upset. It's ok to be concerned. It's ok to be infuriated. It's ok to be tired. But sometimes the only thing that will get you through is knowing God is able. That's why I feel better when I shout out, "Jesus! Have mercy on me!" Even if God doesn't come right then I'm ok because I know God loves me and I know God has the power!

And here's the beauty about God. God states it in God's reply in verse 5. Habakkuk is complaining because of what Habakkuk sees around him (Understandably so). God tells Habakkuk (I'm paraphrasing), "You don't know this but I'm still working." Lord have mercy. I'm making moves. And when you see the moves I'm making, you will utterly amazed. Don't think I don't see this. Don't think I don't notice it. I'm working! And when I finish working, you'll say the same thing as the psalmist in Psalm 13. "I will sing to the Lord because he has dealt bountifully with me."

Can I show you something? We have a social double pneumonia going on. We can't breathe! However, there is a word today for the folk that can't breathe. Today is a special day. Today is Pentecost Sunday. This is the day that celebrates the church starting. It's recorded in Acts 2. The day of Pentecost had come, and they were all together in one place. And suddenly a sound from heaven came like a rushing mighty wind and filled the house. They were all filled with the Holy Spirit and began to speak in other tongues as the Spirit gave the ability.

They were all questioning what was going on because of the different languages spoken in that moment. "What could all of this mean?" There were even some other folks mocking the situation. "These folks must be drunk." Peter stepped up and raised his voice to address what was happening. The people are not drunk. This is to fulfill what was spoken by the prophet Joel. "And it shall come to pass in the last days, that I will pour out My Spirit on all flesh." He said, "And whoever calls on the name of the Lord shall be saved!"

It's Pentecost Sunday. It's the start of the church. It's the moment we celebrate the Spirit breathing on us. In a moment where we're tired and we can't breathe, is the time God says I'll breathe on you. I know it's hard and I know you can't breathe on your own. I know you're tired and I know the proverbial knee has been on your neck for far too long. I'm still God and I'm still here for you. When I can't breathe, God says, "I'll rain on you. I'll breathe on you. I'll shower down and send my Spirit."

This is good news because earlier in Acts 1 Jesus made a profound statement as he was preparing to ascend. In Acts 1:8 he said, "And you shall receive power after the Holy Ghost has come upon you. And you will be my witnesses in Jerusalem, Judea, Samaria, and all over the earth." In other words, when the Spirit breathes on you, the Spirit will give you the power that you need. When the Spirit breathes on you, you'll have the power to make it. When the Spirit breathes on you, you'll be able to represent me throughout the world.

How long Lord? I don't know how long it will be. When will justice come? I don't know when justice will come. But...there is one thing I do know. The Spirit is still breathing and so we still have power! There was a change at Pentecost. The church was born at Pentecost. 3,000 folks made a change at Pentecost. Signs and wonders started happening at Pentecost. Justice came at Pentecost. They had all things in common at Pentecost. They divided their goods among everybody to ensure everybody was taken care of at Pentecost. They praised God! And the Lord added to the church daily those who were being saved.

The power to have the message and ministry of Jesus Christ comes at Pentecost. What is the message and ministry of Jesus Christ? I'm glad you asked. It's summarized in Luke 4. "The Spirit of the Lord is upon me because he has anointed me to preach the gospel to the poor. He sent me to heal the broken-hearted, to proclaim liberty to the captives and recovery of sight to the blind, to set at liberty those who are oppressed, and to proclaim the acceptable year of the Lord." When the Spirit comes, we have power to demand justice. When the Spirit comes, we have power to stand up for those who can't stand for themselves. When the Spirit comes, we can have the courage of Malcolm and the strength of Martin. When the Spirit comes, we can have to drive of Thurgood and the passion of Fannie. When the Spirit comes, we can have the mind of Ella and the will of Bayard. When the Spirit comes, we can have the ambition of Barack and the determination of Maxine.

I know you can't breathe. I know you're wondering, "How long?" Maybe we ought to go back to the basics and build from there. Maybe we ought to take a lesson from the early church and tap into the power of the Holy Spirit to breathe on us when we can't breathe for ourselves. It's Pentecost Sunday and I don't mind calling out, "Spirit of the Living God fall fresh on us!" Call out this Sunday morning! Spirit of the Living God fall fresh on us! Breathe on us! Breathe on us!

Lines Written Upon Reflection on Contemporary Moral Decay

PATRICIA ROBINSON WILLIAMS

Five decades have passed, five scores of years since the prophet of equal
   justice was slain—
And, again, I hear a desperate plea in a voice of pain—
". . .let justice flow like water,
and righteous like an unfailing stream,"
This was the drum major for justice's dream.
Do we see the landscape of righteousness and justice in the dark valley
of contemporary corruption
That snuff out the future of disregarded humanity of the darker hue
And deny that God's image in us is true?
And with a system of pale-colored supremacy
invent a counterfeit democracy?
The time is now to renounce the denial of moral integrity
To view the value of all humanity—
Amid the circumstances of this colossal pandemic
Cast away that which promotes inhumanity as historically systemic.
This presence of moral decay has never welcomed the hope
of heavenly liberation--
But often, in crushing pressure situations, employs oppression.
In such condition light cannot thrive
And the targets of moral decay will not survive—

"There is a river—its streams delight the city of
God, the holy dwelling place of the Most High,
God is within her; she will not be toppled."
The character of human relationships that delights the
Creator of the river
Has yet to convince the so-called earthly power to become a divine viewer
Perceiver of almighty power and influence
Willing to shape circumstances with just governance—
The burden of unjust practices
In which the heaviness of brutal circumstances
Weighs the spirit with an oppressive force
And breathing is no more—
The corporeal frames are suspended
And futures are upended.
Let us conclude that this is but a period framed on a faulty premise,
With a larger purpose in divine providence—
Then may the wailing mothers, wives, grandmothers, cousins and significant
others
Flood the Throne of Grace for grace and mercy for this need
Until evil for goodness will concede.
There is no plea for social deviance to be confirmed
But there is a DEMAND for sanctity of human life to be affirmed.
Surely this moral decay is planting seeds of corruption in human existence—
It is perpetuating genocide
Through deadly minds of homicide—
Cultural blindness
Devoid of moral compliance—
They take as their mission
The timeline of another's earthly commission.
This maltreatment can no longer hold African American manhood in
bondage—
Under enforced restrictions the perpetrators must cease the carnage
Moral decay must relinquish its mantle
And give rise to the liberated gavel!

Contributors

Ristina Gooden is currently a divinity student at Vanderbilt Divinity School where she is concentrating on Black Religion and Cultural Studies as well as Religion, Gender, and Sexuality as well as serving as student government president. She is a licensed Baptist minister on track for ordination. She has a passion for womanism, equity, cultural competency, and community building which is a major part of her work at Faith Matters Network, womanist-led organization focused on personal and social transformation.

Heather Wills is an associate minister at Greater Walters AME Zion Church in Chicago, IL. She holds her Bachelor of Science in Accountancy from the University of Illinois at Urbana-Champaign, her Master of Business Administration from Saint Xavier University, and her Master of Arts in Religious Leadership with a concentration in Social Transformation from Chicago Theological Seminary. Rev. Wills is a union organizer with SEIUHCII, where she organizes healthcare workers to access workplace and economic justice.

Jamar A. Boyd, II is an ordained Baptist minister earning degrees from Georgia Southern University (B.S.) and The Samuel Dewitt Proctor School of Theology at Virginia Union University (M.Div.). He currently serves as the Economic Justice organizer at the Virginia Interfaith Center for Public Policy.

Donna Vanhook is currently an associate pastor at Union Chapel UCC in Burlington, North Carolina. She is also a community organizer and was one of the first four women ordained by the Guilford Educational & Missionary Baptist Association at Elon First Baptist Church of Morgan Place. She earned her M.Div. degree from Shaw University and has been named one of its Distinguished Alumni Preachers.

Howard-John Wesley is the senior pastor of the Alfred Street Baptist Church in Alexandria, Va. He is a fourth-generation Baptist preacher who graduated from Duke University, Boston University School of Theology where he was a Martin Luther King, Jr Scholar, and Northern Baptist Seminary. He is currently pursuing his PhD in African American Preaching and Sacred Rhetoric is the inaugural cohort at Christian Theological Seminary.

Wallis C. Baxter III is the pastor of Second Baptist Church SW in District Heights, MD as well as Vice President of Academic Affairs at Maple Springs Baptist Bible College and Seminary (Capitol Heights, MD). He is a graduate of Morehouse College, Duke Divinity School with an M.Div. Degree, and a 2017 graduate of Howard University with a Ph.D. in African American Literature. Baxter's research interests include the shape of prophetic ministry in 19th-century African American literature and liberation and ethics in America. He is the author of *Phillis Wheatley as Prophetic Poet: You Must be Born Again* (Lexington Books, 2022).

Tamara O. Kersey is a native of North Carolina. She has a BA in English from the University of NC at Greensboro, Master of Technical Communication from East Carolina University (Greenville), and Master of Divinity from Shaw University Divinity School (Raleigh, NC). Tamara is a contributing writer for *The Christian Recorder* and serves as the Associate Pastor of Johnson Chapel AME Church in Mebane, North Carolina.

Aaron X. Marble is the Senior Pastor of the Jefferson Street Missionary Baptist Church in Nashville, Tennessee. Aaron holds a BA and MBA from Xavier University (OH) and a MDiv from Cincinnati Christian University. Prior to the pastorate, Aaron provided human resource management and consultation to three fortune 500 companies.

Andre E. Johnson is an Associate Professor of Rhetoric and Media Studies at the University of Memphis. He is also the Mellon Just Transformation Fellow for the Center of Black Digital Research at Penn State University. He is the author of *No Future in this Country: The Prophetic Pessimism of Bishop Henry McNeal Turner* (University Press of Mississippi, 2020). Dr. Johnson is also senior pastor of Gifts of Life Ministries in Memphis, Tennessee.

Glencie Rhedrick is an ordained Baptist minister and a Womanist Theologian. She currently serves as an associate minister at First Baptist Church-West in Charlotte, North Carolina. She received her Master of Divinity degree with an emphasis in Pastoral Care from the Samuel DeWitt Proctor School of Theology at Virginia Union University in Richmond, Virginia. She also serves as the co-chair of the Charlotte Clergy Coalition for Justice and Social Justice Chair for the United Missionary Baptist Association.

R. Janae Pitts-Murdock serves as Senior Pastor of Light of the Word Christian Church in Indianapolis, Indiana. She is a graduate of the University of Michigan – Ann Arbor with a Bachelor of Arts degree in Communication Studies, Carnegie Mellon University with a Master of Science degree in Public Policy & Management, United Theological Seminary with a Master of Divinity degree, and the University of Memphis with a Master of Business Administration. She is currently a Ph.D. student in the African American Preaching and Sacred Rhetoric program at Christian Theological Seminary.

C. Dexter Wise III is the founding Pastor of Faith Ministries Church in Columbus, Ohio. He earned a BA from the University of Pennsylvania, two Master's degrees from Harvard University and a Doctorate from United Theological Seminary.

Cory Jones is Senior Pastor of Tabernacle Baptist Church of Burlington, New Jersey. He earned a Bachelor of Arts Degree from the University of California, Berkeley, a Master of Divinity from the Morehouse School of Religion at ITC, and a Doctor of Ministry from Beeson Divinity School at Samford University. Currently, he is pursuing a PhD in Marriage and Family Therapy from Eastern University.

Patricia Robinson Williams is an ordained clergywoman, professor, and pastoral psychotherapist. She holds a Ph.D. in English from the University of Illinois-Urbana, M.A. in Pastoral Counseling and Psychology from Houston Baptist University, a doctorate in ministry from Wesley Theological Seminary and a license in marriage and family therapy. She serves as the Minister of Congregational Care and Development at the Wheeler Avenue Baptist Church in Houston, Texas, as well as an adjunct professor at the Houston Graduate School of Theology.

Studies in Communication, Culture, Race, and Religion

Andre E. Johnson, *Series Editor*

Studies in Communication, Culture, Race, and Religion explores and examines the intersection of communication, culture, race, and religion. Books in this series demonstrate how communication and cultural frameworks, helps shape our understanding of race and religion—and in turn, how an understanding of race and religion shapes our understanding of how we communicate and interpret culture. This series will provide space for emerging, junior, or senior scholars engaged in research that studies the intersection of communication, culture, race, and religion to publish exciting and groundbreaking work. Grounded in communication methodology and theory, books in this series will also contribute to our understanding of how communication helps shapes culture and how culture shapes how we communicate. Moreover, this series understands that to further our knowledge of how communication helps to shape culture, an understand of race and religion becomes important. In this series, scholars are open to examine phenomena from either a historical or contemporary perspective and demonstrate how media and culture are intertwined with race and religion. Since these subjects are interdisciplinary, this peer-reviewed book series invites proposals for and submissions of monographs and edited volumes from scholars across all academic disciplines using a plethora of communication methodologies and theories.

For additional information about this series or for the submission of manuscripts, please contact:

editorial@peterlang.com

To order books, please contact our Customer Service Department:

peterlang@presswarehouse.com (within the U.S.)
orders@peterlang.com (outside the U.S.)

Or browse online by series at www.peterlang.com